Turn Your Face

How to Be Heard and Get What You Want Most of the Time

by Barbara J. Linney, MA

Barbara J. Linney, MA
2200 Whilden Court
Charlotte, North Carolina 28221

ISBN: 978-0-9825482-0-2

Library of Congress Card Number: 2009909191

Printed in the United States of America by Lightning Source, Inc.
P.O. Box 503531, St. Louis, MO 63150-3531 615-213-4491

Dedication

To George, Allison, and George III,
the ones I love passionately and who taught me
to step up to the plate and say what I mean.

Acknowledgements

I wrote this book on the weekends over a 12-year period while I had a full time job at the American College of Physician Executives. I write more easily when I have the security of a day job, and I cherish the encouragement and support I get from my colleagues at work. As I have gone down this road, many people have helped me.

My daughter, Allison, was moved by the first part of the title, *Turn Your Face*, because she knew the story about saying it to me when she was two years old. I was still figuring out how to be a good mother, and her request was the beginning of teaching me what I need-ed to know. After I went for counseling when she was five, our relationship improved every year. When I am with her now, we both feel heard, understood, and cared for. She was the first and next-to-last reader and has guided me through the finishing process.

My husband, George, was an early reader. He cheerfully accepts my need for long periods of quiet and has been supportive no matter what stories I told. He has always made me feel he was proud of my growth and accomplishments.

My mother, Ruby Lee, and father, William, thought I could do anything I set my mind to if I worked hard enough at it. Their loving encouragement supported my dreams and lifted me up during difficult times.

Wes Curry, who had been my editor at ACPE for many years, did an early edit and said, "It is good." Eleanor Morton, a close friend did a careful, loving read with many ques-tions and comments and said it was helpful to her. Rachel Brozenske, my daughter's busi-ness partner, gave me the perspective of someone who reads a lot of the books I admire and asked me powerful supportive questions that helped me take the right next step.

My five-year writing group — Diannah Ellis, Gene Owens, and Bill Dols — had parts read to them and told me what they heard the loudest and where they wanted to know more. Roger Schenke, who gave me my first full-time, wonderful job after I had children, heard about it five years ago and regularly asked me in an encouraging way, "How is the book coming?" My *Footprints of the Soul* group heard some of it and said they would like to read more. Mary Kratt, an accomplished writer, listened to the chapter titles and said, "You have your hook."

I gave chapter one to a writing workshop group I did at church and said to myself, "Someone has to say something to me about it or I'm going to quit." Two people did. Ann Cunningham sent me a postcard saying she wanted a copy of the whole book when I finished it. Over lunch Mollie Brugh said positive things.

My early teachers inspired me. Randy Mishoe, who taught me design skills and small group process, was the first person to ask me, "When are you going to write a book?" Sam Watson, a UNCC professor in my master's program, taught me the liberating process of freewriting. Ed St. Clair helped me edit my master's thesis — the longest work I had done up to that point. Irv Rubin and the American Management Association gave me my first traveling-circuit, workshop teacher jobs.

Recent writing teachers - David Whyte, Maureen Ryan Griffin, Debra Moffit and her "Secret Garden" writing groups spurred me on as I was coming down the stretch towards finishing. Bob Kern, a technical writing publisher, said, "Keep going. "

My son, George, III, was the last reader looking for the last typo. He recently finished the heavy reading tasks for a master's at Duke Divinity school and said, "I've never read a book that didn't have at least one mistake." As he often does, he helped me have the courage to let go. His wife, Kristen, was one of the early readers when they were first married, and I didn't know her well. She knew a lot more about me after she finished, and our friendship has continued to grow and flourish.

I didn't always feel I was good at playing when my children were young, but my grandchildren, George IV, Kathryn, and William, have taught me to give myself over completely to their way of playing when I am with them. Being completely absorbed in whatever activity they choose has taught me how to play better in other areas of my life.

Judy Rochell proofed it and helped me with publishing details. Debi Marsh laid it out in book format. Sarah Cramer Shields of Cramer Photo took the cover photo.

Thank you to the many people in workshops who have been willing to do what I asked of them and to my clients who teach me things every day about communicating.

I am grateful to all of you. It wouldn't have happened without you.

Contents

Introduction

I wrote this book because the chapter titles popped into my head when I was writing in my journal on a plane ride to somewhere. I looked at them and thought — yes, these are the things that have taught me to be happy when times are good and to cope better when they are not. During happy times I used to worry about when they would end rather than thoroughly enjoying them. Now I am much better at staying in the present, minding my own business and being content.

My daughter is the reason for the title. When she was little, she started to talk later than most of her playmates, but once she started talking, she didn't stop. I remember preparing dinner while she was talking and she came up to me, tugged at my skirt and said, "Mama, turn your face." She knew I had to stop what I was doing and look at her to listen the way she wanted. The same is true for grown-ups.

My children have had a profound influence on my life. I felt they came from God and had messages for me for how to live my life. When they were little and said things that seemed too wise for their years, I remembered lines from a Wordsworth poem that my mother read to me in high school when I had my head under the bed covers because my eyes hurt from the measles:

> *Our birth is but a sleep and a forgetting:*
> *The Soul that rises with us, our life's Star,*
> *Hath had elsewhere its setting,*
> *And cometh from afar:*
> *Not in entire forgetfulness,*
> *And not in utter nakedness,*
> *But trailing clouds of glory do we come*
> *From God, who is our home:*[1]

---

[1] Wordsworth, William. "Ode: Intimations on Immortality," The Norton Anthology of English Literature, Vol. 2. New York: W. W. Norton & Company, Inc., 1962. p.119.

The story begins when my children were little and continues now that they are adults. My daughter and I both teach communication skills, and she constantly encouraged me to write and helped me edit this book. My son is a graduate of Duke Divinity School. As I have heard him preach and take risks with his writing over the past three years, I have gained courage to put in print my personal stories and words about my own faith.

This book has a lot of my story in it. When I read a book, I want to know what makes the author tick and how she has used what she is recommending. I also give anonymous examples from some of my clients.

When two people turn their faces toward each other, they create a vessel where creativity can happen. I have experienced where "two or more are gathered" God is there if invited. (God is the name I use for a Higher Power. You use the name that works for you.)

When I'm alone and turn my face toward God, paying attention to my inner voice, I come up with creative solutions to problems or a more peaceful way of living without the solution I want. I'll weave back and forth between giving suggestions for things you can try and giving you examples of when I, family members, or people I have worked with have used them successfully.

I write in a journal almost everyday and address the entry to God. I give thanks for the night's sleep and the new day. I talk things over, ask for what I want, and listen for direction for what would be best for my life and those I love. I beg for peace in the world. As I write each morning, I find comfort in organizing my day, clarity about things that need to be said or done, and courage to act. My hope is that this book will help you in the same way.

Chapter 1 (*Write What You Know*) describes an easy, liberating, writing process you can do that helps you feel better. You do not have to be a good writer, speller or grammarian. You just have to be willing to spend ten minutes a day doing it.

Chapter 2 (*Choose What Restores Your Energy*) helps you decide what you like to do and how you can best interact with others. If you get to do enough of what you like to do, you have more energy, communicate better, and give back to the world with sincere gratitude.

Chapter 3 (*Plan What You Want*) gives a process for figuring out what you want. Sometimes we truly don't know what we want, yet we know what we don't want anymore. That's a good place to start.

Chapter 4 *(Listen When you Care)* describes how to listen when you decide to expend the energy. Secretly we all want to be truly known (the good and the bad) and be loved anyway. If someone listens to us without judgment, that can happen. Good listening skills can get you want you want and give others what they want.

Chapter 5 *(Say What You Mean)* is about how to talk so people will want to listen to you, what to do with your body and voice when you talk, how to control your emotions, and why teasing is usually not a good idea.

Chapter 6 *(Work When You Need To)* reminds you that getting what you want takes work. Ideally work that you love, but also a reminder that most successful people started out with some less than ideal jobs.

Chapter 7 *(Control What You Think)* gives concrete suggestions on how to control what goes on in your head. Thoughts influence how you feel and what opportunities come into your life. There are ways to increase the positive and decrease the negative.

Chapter 8 *(Dance When You Can)* reminds you to celebrate life, have fun, give thanks, and give back.

If I live by the chapter titles, I take care of myself, listen for God, and give to others.

Chapter 1

Write What You Know

Grab a pen, put on paper the thoughts in your head as fast as they come to you. Write what you know this day, this minute. The process, called freewriting, is writing without stopping for ten minutes while not worrying about spelling, punctuation, grammar, or content.

Why do it? It can help you feel better, organize your thoughts, find meaning in your life, be kind to your family and friends, contribute value to society, and express gratitude for your life. It can help you get what you want <u>most</u> of the time.

Freewriting, a concept described by Elbow in *Writing Without Teachers*, changed my life. In 1979 I began to write ten minutes every day in a spiral notebook. I was made to do it in my second class in graduate school. It was a class assignment, but it was helping me sort out what was going on in my personal life. I was not coping well with the stresses of two young children. The freewriting helped me see concretely on paper my thoughts and feelings and come up with plans for improvements.

I had a five-year old daughter and a two-year old son. I loved them dearly, but at times I was edgy, hateful — resentful that I no longer talked to educated adults during the day. In my view my husband was not pulling his share of the load at home; however, I wasn't working outside the home, so I thought: "This is my job — why can't I do it better, like it more, be more patient?" As all the discontent, self-pity, and anger spilled onto the page, I began to feel lighter, less depressed. The more I wrote, the more I liked some of the words. New solutions to try for recurring problems kept popping up.

My children are grown now and I have a full-time job, but the activities of work can hurl me along at a pace that causes me to lose sight of important work goals and personal goals. Some days I read and deal with one email after another, answer the phone, check voice mail, return calls, and attend meetings. At the end of the day I can still have over a hundred emails staring at me because they multiplied like rabbits while I was answering other ones. Freewriting can bring all the fragmented, flying around pieces of me back together the way a magnet pulls the little black slivers on an "Etch A Sketch" screen to the center.

When I am rushing through the work day with gnawing anxiety, if I can get myself to sit still long enough to freewrite for five minutes, I can figure out whether I am sad, angry, or scared. The writing can also help me register that I am none of those things. I am just indulging in free-floating worry. Recognizing that, I remind myself to enjoy my good health and happiness.

In the middle of the day, I can grab my journal, take stock of what is going on and decide the next most important thing to do. It might be to leave work and meet a friend for lunch or get back to the project that my boss mentioned first thing that morning. The writing process moves me from a "scattered in all directions" sensation to a "get still and do this" frame of mind.

Freewriting can help you organize your day, get rid of frustration, tap your source of creativity, prepare for important conversations, achieve your goals, and write for work or pleasure if either is required or desired.

How to do it

Freewriting is not regular writing — it is writing without worrying. You pick up a pen, grab some paper, and write whatever thoughts pop into your head. Do it on your computer if you prefer. The process has been given many names — freewriting, practice writing, morning pages, filling your notebook.[2] Freewriting has been my chosen name for the technique for twentysome years because it was such a liberating process for me.

When you freewrite, you write quickly without stopping. You don't worry about spelling, punctuation, grammar, or anything some teacher told you to always remember. If you have such a teacher or other censor that figuratively sits on your shoulder, you want to knock them off and mentally get them out of the room for this exercise. However, there is one catch. You need to start writing and not stop for ten minutes even if you can't think of anything.

[2] In respective order: Peter Elbow, *Writing Without Teachers*, p.3; Natalie Goldberg, *Writing Down the Bones*, p.8; Julia Cameron, *The Artist's Way*, pp.9-18; Gabriele Lusser Rico, *Writing the Natural Way*, pp.21-22.

You can write or type, whichever is easier for you. However, when I type, I tend to correct my mistakes, which causes the editor in me to make judgments. This freewriting process is meant to try to make the judging part of you be still. I know one person who types with his eyes closed and another who turns off the monitor. If writing by hand is tough because you don't do it much, try writing slower, but keep at it for the full ten minutes. If you have to type, go ahead, but I think you will find the exercise more beneficial if you struggle with the writing. The physical act of writing seems to pull more out of your brain.[3]

Sloppy writing is fine. I do not go back and read all my journal entries. However, if I'm writing and suddenly there is good stuff on the page, I put a vertical line in the margin beside those words and later go back and type them into my computer. By good, I mean words that clarified what I was thinking or feeling, or that I want to use in a conversation, or put in a written document or put on a to-do list.

If you write something no one should see, shred it. You do not have to keep it to benefit from having written it.

What to use

Choose your materials carefully. I like to write in a 5-subject spiral notebook, white paper, blue lines, wide rule. I call it a journal. Some people like a bound book with blank pages and a beautiful cover or an 8½ x 14 yellow legal pad. Others like the sound of a clacking typewriter or the softer click of the computer keyboard or the swish of a well-sharpened pencil. Pay attention to what you want, be picky, be ridiculously picky, until you find what suits you.

I write with a cheap Papermate Flexgrip retractable ball-point pen with a comfortable rubberized barrel. This is written on the box and every bit of it matters to me. I want a retractable point so the ink won't get on my purse or collect in the bottom of my pen holder. The rubberized barrel feels good and doesn't slip in my hand. The medium point with blue ink flows smoothly and glides across the page without leaving any blobs. Otherwise, I throw it away. Anytime I have written with an expensive Cross pen, all I can think about is when am I going to lose this pen? It is only a matter of moments. I have twenty cheap pens in a holder on my desk. When I lose one, I just grab another one. At the end of the day I gather them all up and put them back in the holder. If you like an expensive Cross or Waterman pen, get one, get three and use them. Pamper yourself.

---

[3] A participant in one of my seminars said the mechanics of writing or typing are so difficult for some people that speaking into a tape recorder is a better choice. He reminded me the ultimate goal was freeing up your thinking process rather than which technique you use to do it.

When to do it

Early morning is best. You may still have access to your nighttime dreams and your thoughts have not been diluted by conversation. Most days for twenty years I wrote ten minutes of freewriting that was two pages in my spiral notebook. Then I read Julia Cameron's book, *The Artist's Way*. She says write three pages of stream of consciousness writing (another name for this type of writing) every morning. She calls them morning pages and says you must write three of them first thing when you get out of bed.

The ten minutes of writing I had been doing for some time created two pages. Cameron's suggestion caused me to go to three pages. She describes "the page-and-a-half truth point. Many of us find that pay dirt in writing occurs after a page and a half of vamping."[4] The additional page after I had finished whining and complaining gave me more time for creative stuff to appear.

When you first start, try writing any time of the day that you can get yourself to do it. Once I was coaching a man who wanted to write a book. We had talked often about the value of freewriting, but he would not do it. He felt I was a teacher giving an assignment, and he was old enough to refuse. However, he kept coming back to me to talk about how to get started on the book. I asked him, "What is your worst time of day~you are tired, your brain is fried, nothing good can happen?" He said, "4:00pm." I said, "Try freewriting at 4:00pm for a week. You won't be wasting valuable time." He did and got hooked. He wrote the book.

This process is not just valuable for aspiring book writers. If I ask most people if they would like to be more creative, they answer yes, but they think they can't be. All of us have a core of creativity, and this freewriting can be a path to it.

Remember the word creativity doesn't just apply to people who want to write poems and books or paint pictures. It is finding new ways to live your life and do the work that you find satisfying and rewarding. David Whyte in *Crossing the Unknown Sea: Work as a Pilgrimage of Identity* said, "...whatever creative powers we have in our work are intimately connected to our ability to remember who we are amidst the traumas and losses of existence."[5]

---

[4] Julia Cameron, *The Artist's Way*, p.104.
[5] Whyte, *Crossing the Unknown Sea* p.165.

Where to do it

Fix your space. Although you can freewrite anywhere — on planes, in the bathroom, in the car at a stop light, in the dark in bed at night — ideally you would have a special place where you routinely do it. My home office has a twin size bed where I sit so my legs can be propped up with my cocker spaniel at my feet. I have a desk on each side of the bed with a computer on each one. The computer where I do private work is never hooked to the outside world. The other one is connected to my office in Tampa and the Internet. Sitting on that bed or in my office chair, I freewrite three pages almost every morning. There are pictures on the wall that please me, three book shelves that house my most used books, and silk or real red roses in a blue and white vase on a mahogany desk. Pay attention to detail and make it your space.

My office is beautiful but messy. The concept touted by time management experts of touching each piece of paper only once is ludicrous to me. If I did that much organizing, I could never get my job or writing done. I was relieved to read Ned Herrmann in *The Creative Brain* describe my office and say it is a good thing. "Ideally, your creative environment allows you to stop in mid-process with everything spread all over, go away without cleaning up, and come back to pick up exactly where you left off."[6]

However, I know people who can only get work done and be creative in a perfectly neat and maybe even well-decorated space. The place can be a small corner of a bedroom with a screen that surrounds you. The important thing is to figure out what works for you and do it with no apologies to anyone.

Why do it

I write to help myself feel better, to plan what needs to be done that day, to figure out what I want and how to go about getting it. Dr. Phil compares this writing process to a mirror:

> "Thinking through these issues, rather than writing them down, will not work.
> Writing it down adds important objectivity to your self-appraisal. The written word is
> like a mirror. Just as it would be impossible to study your own face without a mirror,
> it is impossible to study your own life without writing it down. Doing so allows you
> to create some objectivity and distance from it."[7]

---

[6] Ned Herrmann, *The Creative Brain*, p.285.
[7] Phillip C. McGraw, *Life Strategies*, p.234.

If I'm not careful, I will give away most of my time and energy and feel guilty about the little bit I have kept for myself, but I also grow angry and resentful. I say "yes, yes, yes" when I should be saying "no, no, no." In the journal I see what I am doing and begin to stop it, begin to say no and get tougher. It helps me feel centered, connected to God and grateful.

I give thanks for my health, for each family member by writing their names; my job, boss and co-workers; the city, country and world I live in. I ask God to bless their lives. I try to visualize each person as well, happy, and doing God's work. I thank God for working in their lives whether I understand what is going on or not.

Sometimes unexpected, surprising messages appear in my journal. Any day I write some words that please me is a good day. No matter how hectic work tasks become I carry with me all day that I accomplished something early in the morning that truly matters to me and that I was called to do.

Writing gives me access to more knowledge than I can pull out of my head by just sitting and thinking. I write more than I know and more than I can remember to say out loud. I first experienced this in undergraduate school. I would study hard for a class but then, once I began to write hard and fast under pressure, I would often write more than I realized I knew. Years later I read Carl Jung's description of the collective unconscious – all wisdom that is out there in the air for any of us to tap into. Looking back, I realized that during those exams I was tapping into Jung's term for universal wisdom, or my term, God. The fast writing process, the desire to fill a certain number of blue books just in case the professor graded on quantity rather than quality made the connection happen. Now forcing myself to write quickly without stopping can make it happen.

What more will free writing do for you?

Freewriting helps you organize your day.

You probably make some kind of "to-do" list. Use the ten minutes to write the list and expand it. Complain about the things you don't want to do.

> Example: Budget re-projections. The numbers literally make me break out in a sweat. Note to Bob. Call doctor to see if he will be advisor to another physician. Wish I could always get into the membership system. Putting in a fire wall keeps me out sometimes but John is great at working to solve the problem. What else?

Decide on travelers for Fall meeting. Evaluation for Janice. There is not enough time in the day, but I stop everything to fill out someone's evaluation because it means money to them.

Complain and keep making the list of what you have to do. When you finish the journal entry, circle the tasks that came up that need to be done that day and assign them numbers in order of importance. You will have a much more complete list than if you just sit and think of one item at a time. By doing the most important things first, you won't feel disappointed at the end of the day because you never got to the urgent tasks.

When I do this, some days it seems I magically do the chores without much effort and without ever looking at the list again. If it's a day with a million interruptions, I keep referring to the list and get back on track when my head feels fuzzy and scrambled.

Freewriting gets rid of frustration.

Anger is a physical phenomenon as well as an emotional, thinking experience. You repeat negative messages in your head but you also feel bodily sensations-knotted stomach, clinched fist, gritted teeth. Name yours. There is no way to avoid anger completely and live with others on this planet, but it is important to get it out of your system for good health. However, you don't want to dump it on the wrong person or kick the dog. You can dump it in your journal. Put down your righteous indignation, filled with curse words, if that is your style. Then tear it up.

Peter Elbow wrote, "Garbage in your head will poison you. Garbage on paper can safely be put in the waste paper basket."[8] It is important that you destroy anything you've written that could harm you. If you momentarily hate your boss, it is helpful to write about it but damaging if anyone sees it. Do not do this on your computer at work or in an email. Neither of these is private no matter what people tell you about passwords and firewalls.

Don't announce to people that you are keeping a journal. The urge to read it may overcome them. Keep the pages safely hidden or tear them up if no one should ever see them. You do not have to keep the words to benefit from having written them.

Freewriting taps your source of creativity.

Have you noticed that as soon as you have a new idea, you often say to yourself — that won't work or I can't have that. By writing quickly without stopping, you can turn off that instant criticism. The censor in our head seems logical and passes judgment on everything we do with the ultimate, primitive goal of trying to keep us alive. Writing these

---

8 Peter Elbow, *Writing Without Teachers*, p.8.

thoughts down can seem scary, but you need to convince yourself that you have control over the words. You can destroy them if they are too dangerous.

If you can keep writing, your muse, the collective unconscious, your Higher Power, God (whatever your name is for that mysterious, spiritual inner voice) will keep sending you fresh ideas because you don't say to it – that was a stupid thought. Some of the ideas will be good and worth acting on. Others will not. You have to get a fair number of ideas on paper to find a few that are good. The best one may pop into your head while showering or driving, but it happens more often when you have been freewriting regularly.

Julia Cameron in *The Artist's Way*, describes art and writing:

> "Art is not about thinking something up. It is about the opposite – getting something down....It is as though all the stories, paintings, music, performances in the world live just under the surface of our normal consciousness. Like an underground river, they flow through us as a stream of ideas that we can tap down into. As artists, we drop down the well into the stream. We hear what's down there and we act on it – more like taking dictation than anything fancy having to do with art."[9]

Freewriting is the bucket for dropping down into the well.

Do not underestimate the fact that whether you are a manager, a stay-at-home mom or dad, a teacher, a nurse, a doctor, an assembly line worker, a lawyer, or a construction worker, you have an artist of some sort within you that needs feeding. Artists can create budgets, build bridges, successfully invest money, and manage the activities of three children. Freewriting can help you find the artist within and do better whatever tasks you do.

Freewriting helps you prepare for important conversations.

While writing in a journal can help prepare you for new, upcoming conversations, I have found it particularly useful for redoing ones that haven't gone well. If you and your boss, co-worker, spouse, or child disagree over the same topic repeatedly, write out the scene in your journal. Often you wish you had said something differently or had not lost your temper. Write the scene the way you wish it had happened. I say... He says.... You will be amazed at how next time the conversation will be similar to what you have written because you are prepared, you have visualized a better interaction, and you stay calm in your half of the conversation.

The first time I used it was in a discussion with my husband about money. At the time, he was making all the money. Since I was at home taking care of young children, he felt

---

[9] Julia Cameron, *The Artist's Way*, p.118.

entitled to make the decisions about how it would be spent. Every time we had this discussion I would get angry, cry, and not be able to get the words out that I wanted to say. I had learned about freewriting, so I wrote the scene out in my journal. I say, he says, etc. I knew what he would say because we had done this on numerous occasions. I put my notes in the bathroom medicine cabinet.

I initiated the discussion. The usual happened, and I could feel the tears coming. I excused myself, went to the bathroom, read my notes, came back, and said what I wanted to say without crying. It did not solve all our tension around money, but it was the beginning of a more equal relationship. We agreed that while I was raising children and not working outside the home, I would have some money that was totally mine to spend without question. If he wanted to make a major purchase, we would discuss it beforehand.

This was one of the first conversations that led to the relationship with him that I cherish today. I was terrified. I thought it would lead to the end of my marriage because less than that had begun the conversation that ended my first marriage.

I have also used the technique to prepare for important and possibly stressful conversations at work. After some layoffs in my organization, the staff met in small groups to offer support and encouragement to each other. One person in a leadership position kept repeating how bad things were. She was right, but I thought she was driving the point into the ground, so I wrote about it and talked to her later. I wrote in my journal to find clarity and courage:

> *"She was so negative, overly negative, bad attitude. So what did she say? We are all overworked since the layoffs and no one cares. She kept saying it over and over. Ok, how many times? 3 times and I felt much worse when the meeting was over. I thought those of us in leadership positions needed to admit how things were but also try to not overstate it, and we needed to look for any bright spots we could find."*

Later I said to her, "In the meeting you said three times — we are all overworked and no one cares. I felt much worse when the meeting was over." Her feelings were hurt and our relationship was strained for a while. But a couple of weeks later, I said to her, "Do you know how much I value you and the work you do? I don't want anything to hurt our friendship." Although that helped begin to smooth things over between us, and she did tone down her complaints about office issues, I needed to speak up even if nothing would change.

Freewriting helps you discover anything else you want to write.

Many people secretly want to write. They dream of poems, novels, short stories, articles, biographies, personal and family stories. Also they have things that need to be written — emails, letters, reports. Red marks from English teachers for years often squelch the longing for personal writing and cause dread about the required writing for work.

The school system (when I was there) generally promoted the notion that you should think before you write and write grammatically correct sentences with no spelling or punctuation errors. That attitude often kills the desire for the secret writing and makes you procrastinate on the requisite writing. A few still long to do it, but as soon as a thought occurs, they judge it in some way — it won't be any good. No one will be interested. I don't have enough research to support the idea. I don't have the time. I just don't want to expend the effort it will take to organize my thoughts.

If you just start writing and suspend the judgment, you can get the basic ideas on paper and then have something to work with. More ideas will come to you if you keep writing than if you just sit and think.

Natalie Goldberg calls the process "writing practice" and compares it to drawing:

> "A friend once said that when she had a good black-and-white drawing that she was going to add color to, she always practiced first on a few drawings she didn't care about in order to warm up. This writing practice is also a warm-up for anything else you might want to write. It is the bottom line, the most primitive, essential beginning of writing. The trust you learn in your own voice can be directed then into a business letter, a novel, a PhD dissertation, a play, a memoir. But it is something you must come back to again and again. Don't think, 'I got it. I know how to write. I trust my voice. I'm off to write the great American novel.' It's good to go off and write a novel, but don't stop doing writing practice. It is what keeps you in tune, like a dancer who does warm-ups before dancing or a runner who does stretches before running. Runners don't say, 'Oh, I ran yesterday, I'm limber.' Each day they warm up and stretch."[10]

If I have a writing task that needs to be completed, I often begin in my journal by complaining about how much I don't want to do it. This is after I have exhausted all other modes of procrastination — dusting the hall chandelier, cleaning the toilet, getting dirt and dog hair out of the crevice where the carpet meets the wall. After I moan and whine in a freewriting style, suddenly the words I need begin to pour onto the page. I put a vertical line beside them in the margin, then go back and type them into my computer after I

---

[10] Natalie Goldberg, *Writing Down the Bones*, p.13.

finish my 15 minutes of freewriting. This morning writing exercise helps me write work assignments during the week and pleasure writing on the weekend. It's as if the wheels of the machinery (my brain and hand) have been oiled.

Remember to suspend judgment. If you can't decide which of three words you like, write them all down without taking time to decide which one fits best. Don't look up how to spell a word. Just put <u>sp</u> above it and keep writing. If you can't decide whether to use who or whom, he/him or she/her, put both down and keep writing. It is important not to trigger the editing impulse when you are generating ideas. Here's an example of freewriting that has short to-do list sentences:

> So I wake up at 5:30 or 6:00. Can't remember which. One of those times each morning. It's 7:00 and I have 2½ pages that are pretty decent. It's 7:00am. Walk, take Rusty to the vet, pack, curl hair. Continue to clean up office. Read paper maybe. Call man about pine needles. I have 7 bales left over. Tell them to come next Wed. So I planted the roses. I feel good. A lot has happened this week. So keep writing. Talk about the reading part. Read the kind of literature you want to write. Think of the titles later. They already know everything about reading.

Here's an example that has a longer "figure out what is going on" sentence that lends a little poetry to my malaise. Whenever that happens, I feel more satisfied:

> I am tired. The azaleas and dogwoods are at their peak. I adore looking at them, but the pollen they bring usually causes a slack-jawed, stare-into-space lethargy that makes me wonder if I have always been this lazy and if so what have I done to combat it in the past. Ah – it's time to up the antihistamines.

Freewriting can help you empty out interfering feelings when you need to get a writing project done. Elbow describes the many reasons we have for putting off writing:

> "We have lots in our heads that makes it hard to think straight and write clearly: We are mad at someone, sad about something, depressed about everything. Perhaps even inconveniently happy. 'How can I think about this report when I'm so in love?' Freewriting is a quick outlet for these feelings so they don't get so much in your way when you are trying to write about something else. Sometimes your mind is marvelously clear after ten minutes of telling someone on paper everything you need to tell him."[11]

---

[11] Peter Elbow, *Writing With Power*, p.15.

Freewriting helps you set and achieve goals.

Dr. Lee Poulos in *The Power of Visualization* audiotapes says only 4% of the population write down their goals. Those who do write them down achieve them almost 100% of the time.[12] When you write out a goal, you think it with your brain, write it with your hand, and see it with your eyes. Then your subconscious and the universe plan ways to make it happen.

Often people are afraid to write down their goals because if they do not accomplish them, they will feel the failure more intensely. Try to let that go. You can keep the goals secret. You can tear them up and even forget them. Sometimes I keep goals where I can see them — other times not. Either way, many goals that I've written down have come true. There is mysterious power in the writing of them.

When I keep my goals visible, I use freewriting to help me keep my focus on them. If I feel overwhelmed with too many tasks, I will write the answers to these questions:

- Is this what I want to be doing?
- Does this move me toward my goal?
- What is that nagging irritation?
- Can I do anything about it now? If the answer is no, then putting it on paper releases me from using energy trying to remember it or trying to forget it. I can deal with it later and get back to working on my daily goal during the work week or personal long-term goal on the weekend.

I'll talk much more about how to use freewriting for goal setting in Chapter 3. As the book progresses, you'll see even more ways this writing process can help you:

- be more innovative and productive at work
- improve your relationships by enhancing your communication skills
- think of fun activities to do
- achieve more balance in your life and be more satisfied with your choices
- foster a sense of peace and well being.

12 Lee Pulos, PhD, The Power of Visualization.

Sometimes I won't freewrite

I've given lots of reasons to freewrite in a journal, and it helps in most situations but, in my experience, not all. When my father was dying and when I was recovering from surgery that had not corrected a problem were two times I couldn't stand to see proof of my misery in print. Things had to improve some before I could freewrite again.

In ordinary times with smaller problems, such as a cold or flu, freewriting can eventually help me. At first I wallow in self pity and say things such as: my head is splitting, my throat feels like it's been cut, I am going to explode with this cough. As soon as I have the strength to sit up, I start writing, "I am happy and healthy." If I write it enough, I begin to say it in my head when I am walking around, even when going to the bathroom in the middle of the night. It is healing.

Most of the time I will freewrite

In everyday life, when I frequently choose to worry because it is my natural tendency or when I get so busy with work that I can't remember why I am working in the first place, writing 15 minutes each morning helps me calm down, remember my blessings, thank God, and focus on what I want and need to do. On weekends or vacations, I write and write and write until I feel filled. Sometimes the words are sniveling, pitiful, meaningless whining. Sometimes they are great and just what I need to know for that day. Often the process empties out what I don't want to think or feel and fills me with wisdom, faith, and courage.

My grown daughter, an organizational development consultant, heard me talk about freewriting for 15 years before she would try it. After three years of doing it, she said, "It helps me clear the junk out of my head, begin my day well, prepare for interactions and plan what I need to do. I don't want to write a book right now, but I do want to write good proposals and emails. I want most of all to talk with people effectively. It helps me get control of foot-in-mouth disease. It's the place where I deal with emotions that can be uncomfortable to me. It's talking to God. I don't know what it will be. I come to freewriting with no agenda; I don't do that very often in other areas of my life. I have explored a lot of time and stress management tools for myself and clients — it's the best way I know to have a meaningful and productive day."

So pick up the writing utensil of your choice and write what you know for this day. Some days you will know more and other days less, but put down your thoughts, feelings, questions, and answers for right now. It will help you think better, feel better, communicate better, and enhance your creativity.

Works Cited

Cameron, Julia. *The Artist's Way: A Spiritual Path to Higher Creativity*. New York: Jeremy P. Tarcher/Putnam, 1992.

Elbow, Peter. *Writing With Power*. New York: Oxford University Press, 1981.

Elbow, Peter. *Writing Without Teachers*. New York: Oxford University Press, 1973.

Goldberg, Natalie. *Writing Down the Bones*. Boston: Shambhala Publications, 1986.

Herrmann, Ned. *The Creative Brain*. Lake Lure, North Carolina: Brain Books, 1990.

McGraw, Phillip C. *Life Strategies*. New York: Hyperion, 1999.

Pulos, Lee, PhD. *The Power of Visualization* (Audiotapes). Niles, Illinois: Nightingale-Conant Corporation, 1993.

Rico, Gariele Lusser. *Writing the Natural Way*. Los Angeles: J.P. Tarcher, 1983.

Whyte, David. *Crossing the Unknown Sea: Work as a Pilgrimage of Identity*. New York: Riverhead Books, 2001.

Chapter 2

Choose What Restores Your Energy

I took a giant step toward self-acceptance when I learned there was nothing wrong with me because I wanted a weekend alone with no threat of anyone interrupting it. The Myers-Briggs Type Indicator[13] taught me that. It also showed me other ways I could choose what I like and be energized, restored, and strengthened to go back into the world and be a valuable, contributing member of society.

The writing described in Chapter 1 is a private activity. Now we'll begin to think about interacting with others. Understanding your needs and then choosing what you like in order to take care of yourself is the first step in getting along with others.

Initially it may seem selfish, but if you don't nurture yourself, you have nothing to give others. If you continue to give long after you want to, long after you should have stopped, long after you needed rest, you will become resentful and eventually sick.

The Myers-Briggs Type Indicator can help you figure out what you like.[14] I've known people who were exposed to its concepts and turned off by them. However, I hope to give you just enough information to be useful to you, but not overwhelm you, because it has been one of the most important tools I have used as an adult. It has helped me accept who I am, understand my own communication style and make educated guesses about others' styles so I can more effectively listen and sometimes influence them. It has given me a framework for discovering what I want and permission to go after it. It renews my energy so I am motivated to give to others. For those wanting more in-depth information, I'll list several books at the end of this chapter.

---

13 The Myers-Briggs Type Indicator is an assessment tool that helps you decide what behaviors you prefer in many life situations.

14 I think you can get the gist of the Myers-Briggs information in this chapter, but you need to talk to someone to verify your type. I hope to whet your appetite and encourage you to do more. You can contact CAPT, Center for Applications of Psychological Type, 800-777-2278, http://www.capt.org/take-mbti-assessment/mbti.htm to take the assessment.

The Myers-Briggs Type Indicator is based on the work of Carl Jung, a late 19th and early 20th century psychiatrist, who "...believed we are born with a predisposition to certain personality preferences."[15] Katherine Briggs had been devising her own classification of personality differences when she read Jung's work and realized that their theories were similar, but his were more thoroughly developed.

> "In 1942, prompted by World War II...and the conviction that the war was caused, in part, by people not understanding differences," Katherine Briggs and her daughter, Isabel Myers "began to develop a series of questions to measure personality differences. The result was the Myers-Briggs Type Indicator."[16]

Their work, combined with Jung's, identified four pairs of opposite behaviors to describe how people usually act if they have the freedom to choose.

When you fill out and score the instrument, you come up with a set of four letters out of a possible 16 combinations. They are based on eight behaviors. I'll briefly describe each behavior in hopes that you will be able to say, "Yes, I'm somewhat like that one but not so much like that one," and then perhaps you will want to pursue the information further. The four pairs of behaviors are:

(E) Extravert   Introvert (I)

(S) Sensing   Intuition (N)

(T) Thinking   Feeling (F)

(J) Judging   Perceiving (P)

The four pairs of behaviors describe our source of energy, how we take in information from the world, how we make decisions about the information we have taken in, and how we organize our lives. As you are deciding which behavior you prefer, keep in mind that everyone exhibits all eight behaviors, but most people prefer one in each pair more than the other — sometimes a little and sometimes a lot.

Discovering which set of letters you like best and arranging your life so you cater to your preferences at least some of the time can increase your energy and make you feel more satisfied with your life. Overdoing any of your preferred letters for too long can lead to exhaustion or interpersonal conflicts, so knowing when to back off from a certain behavior can improve your health and communication with others.

---

15 Kroeger and Thuesen, Type Talk, p.281.

16 Kroeger and Thuesen, p.282.

Extravert and Introvert

This first pair (Extravert and Introvert) explains our source of energy. Try to forget society's definition of the two words — outgoing and shy. Jung used them differently.

Extraverts get energy from people and activities outside themselves. They want to talk to others a lot, often working out their thoughts aloud as they talk. If they've had a hard day, they usually want to talk it over with someone to debrief and restore themselves.

Introverts get energy from being quiet, going within themselves, having an internal dialogue. They usually need a fair amount of time alone and prefer to do their thinking quietly by themselves and then let others know what they have worked out. If they are tired, have been with people too much, they need solitude to recover.

I am an Introvert. My husband is an Extravert. We do a lot of business travel. Sometimes we teach a seven-hour seminar together. We're both tired at the end of that day, but we try to renew ourselves in different ways. When we are waiting for the plane to take us home, he will walk to the gates of all the places he has lived, looking for people he knows that he can talk to. I check in, sit down, open a book, and don't look up until it is time to board the plane. I don't want to talk to anyone. Neither way is right or wrong — just different.

At cocktail parties, sometime during the evening I go sit in the bathroom for five minutes. I need an alone time break to get energy to go back and carry on with small talk. I've been doing this for years with only my family members knowing what was going on. They laugh with me about this, but ultimately they understand it is one of the many ways I take care of myself.

I resonated with Marti Olsen Laney when I read in *The Introvert Advantage* the description of her bathroom experience at the beginning of party.

> *"The room is a sea of people. The loud voices hurt my ears. I scan the room for a safe nook. My stomach tightens. My breath quickens. I feel like retreating. My husband, Mike, sees friends he wants to say hello to. He's smiling and nodding all the way. That's when I make a beeline for the bathroom. I stay in there, checking out the wallpaper, the hand towels, and the soap. I really appreciate a well-appointed bathroom. I begin to relax. My stomach unclenches. My breathing returns to normal. After a while, I feel prepared to leave the sanctuary of the bathroom. I locate Mike's bald spot in one of the huddled groups. I slip in beside him. He hands me a Pepsi. I chat with people. I enjoy hearing what they have to say. It's fun to laugh and talk."*[17]

---

[17] Laney, *The Introvert Advantage*, p.159.

I know Extraverts who are so energized by the cocktail party that they will ask six or eight people to go out to dinner afterwards.

People are wired differently. To refuel or increase your energy level, you need to get to do your preferred way some of the time.

Extraverts and Introverts can annoy each other, but they can also enjoy what the other offers. I met my husband on a blind date. It was my first date after my first marriage ended. When I am extremely nervous, I can't talk. Words whirl around in my head, but I think they sound stupid so I just sit there. He is an Extravert. He didn't stop talking for 45 minutes. It was wonderful. By then I had something intelligent to say. Even when I can't talk, I can listen well, and he still appreciates that after more than 30 years.

Extraverts begin to talk and then, seven or eight sentences later, they know where they stand on an issue because they do their best thinking out loud. Introverts sometimes believe Extraverts have lied to them at the beginning of the conversation, but it's not necessarily so. They are working through a problem by talking, while the Introvert would do all their thinking internally and then deliver a finished product. Extraverts can be equally annoyed with Introverts because they resent that Introverts didn't let them in on any of their quiet thinking process.

Kroeger and Thuesen write:

> "If you are an Extravert, you tend to talk first, think later, and don't know what you'll say until you hear yourself say it....you probably know a lot of people and count many of them among your 'close friends'....If you are an Introvert, you probably rehearse things before saying them and prefer that others would do the same....you like to share special occasions with just one other person or perhaps a few close friends."[18]

Many Introverts get nervous when people come to their homes. It is such an invasion of their private space. They fear they won't measure up, that people will learn their inner secrets. I might forget to put out the guest towels or check to see if there was soap in the bathroom. Or worse — my dog will poop in the hall. That happened once, but my husband found it and cleaned it up before anyone saw.

Judith Provost explains why Introverts and Extraverts feel differently about entertaining:

> "...for Introverts, home is often a sanctuary, a place to renew oneself away from the busy pace of the world. Their extraverted partners, on the other hand, may wish to have friends drop in frequently or may prefer the activity and stimulation of going out more often than Introverts do."[19]

---

18 Kroeger and Thuesen, *Type Talk*, pp.14-15.

19 Judith Provost, *Work, Play and Type*, p.76.

During courtship, people are often attracted to their opposite behavior on some and sometimes all the letters. We unconsciously think that person could bring those missing qualities into our lives. Then, when we marry or start living with them, those once charming traits begin to grate on our nerves. It is a new day for couples if they can learn to not be irritated by their differences, remember why the differences were attractive in the first place, and even help each other do what they need to do.

Under extreme stress Extraverts talk too much and say things they may regret, Introverts become silent and think of what they wish they had said two hours to two days later. I have not read or experienced anything that shows those tendencies can be changed, but there are actions that Extraverts can take to have more control during the moment and things Introverts can do before and after the fact to improve a situation. Both have to prepare and both have to sometimes clean up afterwards.

Writing can help both types prepare. If an Extravert writes out everything she wants to say, she can sometimes make judicious decisions about what to leave out when she talks. The Introvert can get lots of words on the page and remember enough of them during the conversation to make his point convincingly. Speaking into a tape recorder and listening to how you sound is also a good way to prepare.

If an interaction didn't go well, the Extraverts can sincerely apologize and try to set things straight. Introverts can open up the conversation again and say, "I have more to say on the topic we were discussing."

Here are some snippy retorts I wrote in my journal a day after my feelings were hurt in two separate conversations:

> "I am so angry that in your pissed-ness you messed up the disk and destroyed three hours of work that I did while I was trapped at your place."

> "I was hurt, then angry when you said, 'I'm glad you are not going to be board chair if you get nervous arranging flowers.'"

Sometimes I say these things. Sometimes I don't. Writing them down releases me from the anger and the constant rumination of the phrase, "I can't believe s/he said such and such." If change is really necessary, then I muster up my courage and go have the conversation.

My daughter is an Extravert. Stress can be lowered for her if she can vent and tell me all the things that have aggravated her. As an Introvert, I first need to be alone to sort things out, regain equilibrium but then it helps to tell her what has been bothering me. She is my close friend so my stress can be lowered by describing the situation and trusting her not to tell it.

Again, please remember, we all do both kinds of behaviors. My daughter, who has a strong preference for extraversion, spends two weekend days in total solitude with only her dog to recover from a string of hectic working days. Extraverts eventually need some alone time to restore themselves.

And Introverts eventually need to be with others or they can sink into too much depressing worry. Introverts gain energy by being alone as long as they have some important people in their lives who desire their company. If they don't, they get lonely like everyone else.

Before you read about the next set of behaviors, write the answers to the following questions. Which term seems to describe how you like to do things and restore your energy? Extravert or Introvert? Is your life structured so you can do enough of this behavior to satisfy you? If not, how could you make some changes?

Sensing and Intuition

The second set of letters, S and N for Sensing and Intuition, describes how we take in information about our world. You're inside your skin. The world is out there. You need to take in information about that world. Sensing types take in information through their five senses — what they see, hear, smell, taste and touch. Intuitives take in information through a sixth sense, a hunch. They think they know something and are not sure why, but they are right often enough that they come to trust their hunches.

Sensing types like to work with details, and they approach projects in a step-by-step manner, starting at the beginning and proceeding until they are finished. They like established ways of doing things. Because they don't mind repetition, their motto might be, "If it isn't broken, don't fix it."

S's read and follow directions and think everyone would if they were reasonable. N's read directions as a last resort. They much prefer looking at a picture or visualizing what the finished product would look like and then trying to construct it. If they have ten parts left over when they finish, but the object works, they don't care. If the object doesn't work, they will probably find an S and sweet talk or pay them to take it apart and put it together again following the directions.

Whereas Sensing types are very comfortable with proven methods, Intuitives rarely like to do the same thing twice. They start big projects, sometimes tackling the middle section first and skipping around from one idea to the next without a particular order. Intuitives see the big picture. They are often looking toward the future and imagining possibilities. Details sometimes overwhelm, exhaust, or bore them whereas Sensing types often trust and are comforted by details.

Intuitive types often like executive positions where they are responsible for long-range planning, designing new services, or solving unexpected problems. They frequently serve in counselor roles no matter what titles they have because they enjoy helping people think of possible changes they might make in their lives.

Sensors often enjoy work where procedures need to be established, attention to detail is mission critical, and a step-by-step approach is valued. Many who launch the space shuttles are probably S's.

If you show a peanut to Sensing types, they see a small brown object, two round shapes joined together, maroon flaky stuff on the inside, tan nut, tastes good. The outside covering looks like it might be bumpy and rough, but they would like to touch it to confirm that. Show a peanut to Intuitive types and their response might be — Jimmy Carter raised peanuts; George Washington Carver did experiments on peanuts; I like Reeses peanut butter cups; I fixed a peanut butter and jelly sandwich this morning for my child. They will think of something beyond what they are actually looking at. Intuitives will want to know — what's the peanut's potential? What can you do with it?

Kroeger and Thuesen wrote about attitude of S's and N's toward time and money:

> *"If you are a Sensor, you probably prefer specific answers to questions; when you ask someone the time, you prefer 'three fifty two' and get irritated if the answer is 'a little before four' or almost time to go....If you are Intuitive, you probably would rather fantasize about spending your next paycheck than sit and balance your checkbook."*[20]

These two types often get on each other's nerves because their styles are different, but if they can work together without driving each other crazy, good things happen. The Intuitives imagine and start some great projects, and the Sensing types help them finish them, tending to many of the details. Each needs the other. They can make wonderful things happen if they both sincerely respect the other.

---

[20] Kroeger and Thuesen, *Type Talk*, pp.18-19.

In 1987 I asked my mother, who is an S, if she would write down the names of my grand-parents and their parents as far back as she could remember so I could tell my children when they asked me. The question prompted her to buy a computer and spend the next five years researching our genealogy. She poured over court records, went to cemeteries, took pictures of tombstones and spent hours in the library. She did it because she loved the details of the research, the information she discovered and the brain stimulation. My father, an Extravert and an Intuitive, enjoyed the trips they took and the people they met but never was interested in the details about who was related to whom four generations back.

I want to remind you that we all use all of the behaviors because at this point in my seminars, people will say, "But I do both." They are right. Work will usually require all the behaviors and recreational activities can need them.

It is always easier to get yourself to use your less preferred letter if you are doing it in service to your preferred letter.

For example, I use both N and S for many of the activities I love to do — decorating, sewing, designing educational programs for work. Here are some examples where I start out using my preferred letter (N) and then follow up with S activities to get the task completed.

First example:

I love to picture over and over how a room will look as I decorate it (N), then run around finding the many pieces that make it work (S), looking for the absolute best bargain but spending enough to make it exactly the way I want. The process can boost my energy level, even keep me awake at night if I'm not careful. I mentally go to every part of the room, seeing the forest green color of the 90-inch round table cloth I'll put on a decorator table with glass top, the placement of an oil painting on the wall with dishes hung on each side. How the table, drapes, and bedspread will look elegant against the light gray paint of the walls. (N)

Second example:

I did a lot of sewing in the first years of marriage. Sewing is an (S) function but I would always visualize (N) how the garment would look, how trim I might look in it, how the color would brighten my complexion, how people might compliment me on the dress and be amazed that I made it. In the meantime I sewed one seam and one stitch at a time. (S)

Third example:

> I design programs on communication skills and creativity as a part of my job. I imagine how people will react to the facts and stories I tell them. Then I use (S) skills to create a sequential power point presentation with helpful handouts.

So again, we all use all the behaviors, but usually prefer one in each set, sometimes a little and sometimes a lot.

Which term seems to describe how you like to do things, how you like to take in information, Sensing or Intuitive? Is your life structured so you can do enough of this behavior to satisfy you? If not, how could it be?

Thinking and Feeling

The two sets of behavior, Thinking and Feeling, explain how people prefer to make decisions about the information they have taken in. Thinking types make decisions based on what is logical and reasonable. Feeling types consider how the decision will affect other people and themselves. Try to put aside society's definition of these two terms because Thinking types feel and Feeling types think. The Myers-Briggs theory uses the terms to describe how they prefer to make decisions.

Thinking types are good at analyzing and solving problems. They are often firm and tough-minded and may hurt people's feelings without realizing it. If it makes economical sense to fire someone, they can do it without agonizing over the decision. They think logically about cause and effect if a change is made — What will be the result? What will it cost? Who will we need to hire or fire? How will the work flow be affected? How will this be fair to others?

Whereas thinking types decide with their heads, feeling types decide with their hearts. They suffer when they have to fire people because they worry about hurting feelings and causing hardship. Feeling types are good at understanding people. They like harmony and are willing to work to make it happen or restore it when things go awry. They think about how people will feel if a change occurs.

Kroeger and Thuesen described how T's don't always need friends at work, but F's prefer to have them:

> *"If you are a Thinker, you probably think it's more important to be right than liked; you don't believe it is necessary to like people in order to be able to work with them and do a good job....If you are a Feeler, you probably put yourself in other people's*

moccasins; you are likely to be the one in a meeting who asks, 'How will this affect the people involved?'"[21]

Yet, it's important to remember that Thinking types feel and Feeling types think. Thinking types care deeply about family, friends, and causes and Feeling types are astute at knowing what action will cause predicted results. I am pointing out their most natural comfort zones as I describe them.

My mother lives in a nearby retirement community, and we talk regularly. She is a T, and I am an F. We have always been good friends, but at times I am astonished at her matter-of-fact acceptance of tough situations, and she is amazed at my hurt feelings and inability to sleep when tragic events occur. It is an artful dance for each of us to accept the other in this area and not think the other one is wrong. We are just different even if the same blood courses through our veins.

She loves numbers. She watches the stock market tape run across the bottom of her TV screen three to four times a day on the business channel. When she is stressed or sick, she will start quoting numbers to me — glucose levels, blood pressure, numbers of a kidney function test, stock and bond prices. These numbers and logical reasons for her illness comfort her.

Several years ago she gave me some stock and at tax time she was going to help me understand how to report the earnings. She is very kind about it, never makes fun of me, and says she didn't know anything about the stock market before she retired and couldn't even read the quotes in the newspaper. She said, "You can learn it when you have time to study it." I was listening to her explanation with all the brain power I could muster and then after five minutes my head felt as if it were full of cotton candy. I couldn't understand what she was saying and at the end of it, I realized she had read me a whole page of numbers that I did not need to know. I thought, "She has no idea what a negative effect that has on me because those numbers are very comforting to her."

When the war in Iraq began, to cope she needed to watch TV, see what was going on and then go to sleep. Analyzing the information about a bad situation can calm her. I needed to not see the TV images because they kept me awake, or they permeated my dreams in a restless sleep. I read the paper, but just enough of it to not be embarrassed in public when the topic was discussed. When I read the paper, I can decide to control the intake of information. When I watch TV, it feels like the visual images penetrate to my bone marrow. Then I am not useful to myself or others.

---

21 Kroeger and Thuesen, *Type Talk*, p. 19.

Manny Elkind, a friend and fellow communications consultant, says something physiological happens in your brain when you are receiving information that is different from your preferred style. That doesn't mean you can't or shouldn't do it, because we can learn from trying different styles; it makes us more flexible and compassionate when interacting with others. Just remember it is taxing, takes more energy, and can feel overwhelming. Plan ways to reward and restore yourself afterward.

Before you read about the next set of behaviors, write the answer to the following questions: Which term seems to describe how you like to do things, how you like to make decisions, Thinking or Feeling? Do you get to do enough of this behavior to satisfy you? How do you or how could you structure your life so you meet the need of this letter?

Judging and Perceiving

The labels Judging (J) and Perceiving (P) describe how you organize your life. Judging types like to make decisions and get things settled quickly, giving them a sense that they have life under control. Perceiving types like to continue to take in more information and keep their options open without the feeling of being tied down to a schedule.

Isabelle Myers and her son, Peter, wrote in *Gifts Differing*:

> *"Judging types live according to plans, standards, and customs not easily or lightly set aside, to which the situation of the moment must, if possible, be made to conform. Perceptive types are frequently masterful in their handling of the unplanned, unexpected, and incidental, but may not make an effective choice among life's possibilities."[22]*

"Most of us have to behave like Judgers at least part of the time, particularly at work. If you have a demanding job, you have to get there on time, meet deadlines and make lots of decisions."[23] Perceivers are flexible and respond well to change. Both qualities are needed in the workplace.

I am a P when I relax but have some strong J qualities when I teach. I am a fanatic about starting and stopping on time and getting the material in the notebook covered because I know participants are happiest when they receive all the information they paid for.

---

[22] Myers and Myers, *Gifts Differing*, p.75.

[23] Tieger and Barron-Tieger, *Do What You Are*, p.29.

I work closely with a J who gets excited about adding order to an unruly group of papers that are generated in a program we do together. She likes putting them in colored folders in a way that makes them easy for a committee to review. She also reorganizes her clothes closet every six months, sells what she no longer likes and buys new clothes with the proceeds.

> "If you are a Judger, you probably thrive on order; you have a special system for keeping things in the refrigerator and dish drainer, hangers in your closets, and pictures on your walls....If you are a Perceiver, you don't believe that 'neatness counts,' even though you would prefer to have things in order; what's important is creativity, spontaneity, and responsiveness."[24]

J's almost always know where their shoes are. P's think somewhere in the house is close enough. P's don't believe everything has a place and it should be there. J's do think that kind of order is necessary for good thinking and quality living and mumble under their breaths that P's are slobs. P's will mumble about J's inability to relax.

My husband is a J and I am a P. If we have a rest day coming up – a Saturday where neither of us travels for work, and we can spend it any way we want, we have a very different approach. He knows on Monday that at 9:45am on Saturday he is going to tee off at the golf course with his three favorite golfing buddies. He wants the golf round to take four hours or less. He'll come home, fix himself some lunch, watch specific, preplanned sporting events on TV and go out to dinner with me that night.

I am a P. If I know on Monday what I'm doing on Saturday, it is already ruined. I don't want to have any planned commitments. I want to wake up when I feel like it, get some breakfast, might go to my office and read or write a little, might paint, knit or sew. I might go to a mall – if I'm there five minutes and don't like the feel of it, I'll go home or go to another mall. There is no one along to say, "Well that was a stupid decision. Why did you waste the time and gas to come here?" I bounce from activity to activity all day long as the thoughts occur to me, and I know I'm going out to dinner with my husband that night. I do J things all day every day in my work, but if I want to restore myself, a carefree unplanned day is what I need.

Our children are grown so we get to make these kinds of decisions about how to spend a rest day. What can happen in many households is that on Saturday morning, the J wakes up with a list of things for the P to do and a schedule for the day. Then there is some discord. Each thinks the other is a lower life form. They may call each other names – quietly

---

[24] Kroeger and Thuesen, *Type Talk*, p.21.

in their heads and sometimes out loud. The J will think the P is a lazy goof-off and the P may think the J is a control freak. If they can each come to accept that the other one needs to restore him or herself in a different way, they can find ways to get both their needs met without wasting the energy of being critical or arguing. They could take turns on how they will do things on Saturday.

Which term seems to describe how you like to do things, Judging or Perceiving? Is your life structured so you can do enough of this behavior to satisfy you? How do you or how could you structure your life so you meet the need of this letter?

Why Bother to Think About Preferences?

Knowing about your preferences can help you take care of yourself on a regular basis and find a solution to stress when you are in trouble. It also helps you communicate better with others and influence them when you need to.

Taking Care of Your Self.

Soren Kierkegard's words have strongly influenced me: "This then is the formula which describes the condition of the self when despair is completely eradicated: by relating itself to its own self and by willing to be itself the self is grounded transparently in the Power which posited it."[25] Simply put, a Self that comes to know itself and then chooses itself is grounded transparently in God. The choosing is a huge step and one that people often don't do. Many come to know what they prefer but then do not stand up for themselves and ask for it or demand it. If you do not take care of yourself first, you do not have energy and quality time to give to anyone else.

So if you come to know yourself and choose yourself, find out what you prefer and then do those things, at that point you are grounded in God. I am not talking about self-abusive behaviors. If you want excessive amounts of alcohol and drink it, that is not good for you, and ultimately not choosing yourself. I mean self-enhancing behaviors that are your choice — not someone else's choice for you.

Think about each of your preferred letters. Are you getting to do enough of that behavior? If not, change something about your life. Even a small change can make a difference. If you decide which behaviors you prefer and structure your life so you get to do them, you will find you have more energy, you can more easily choose work and play that satisfies you.

[25] Soren Kierkegard, *Fear and Trembling and the Sickness Unto Death*, p.147.

Here is a list of activities that will help you choose yourself and take care of yourself using your Myers-Briggs Type Indicator information:

- **Extraverts** — Plan activities to be with people. Call them on the phone. Brainstorm out loud with people. Talk to a family member or friend to figure out what you think and feel about your life and work. Go for a run in a group. Go to the gym where the sound and action of other people, even TV, will energize you as you exercise.

  I talked to one Extravert, who while writing a book, scheduled lunch or meetings with friends after work several times a week to meet his need to be with people.

- **Introverts** — Plan to have time alone. Get caller ID and don't answer the phone unless you want to. Quietly think through a conversation you would like to have or write about it. Be alone so you can hear your own thoughts and God. Write in your journal until you feel emptied out of stress and filled up with gratitude, stillness.

  If you are a two-career household with children, every other day for an hour or one day of the weekend at least once a month, arrange for the other to go away and be alone or be home alone. One Introvert asked his wife if he could go sit by the lake in their subdivision for 15 minutes before he came home.

- **Sensing** — Do something that lets you have control over details. Write computer programs. Have a detailed filing system. Plan an elaborate dinner. Alphabetize your CDs or books. Take a quilting class. Do your own taxes using the latest tax software program or organize the W-2, 1099s and receipts for your accountant.

- **Intuition** — Use your imagination to come up with new projects. Have a capture system. Write them down or carry a small cassette recorder with you, or type them into your Blackberry. Try to carry out some of them. Paint with oils or acrylics whether you think you can paint or not — take a class. Picture a room in the house decorated in a new way, imagine how a visit with a grandchild could go — arranging boxes, spoons, toys he or she might want to play with. Fantasize about things you hope to achieve in 5, 10, or even 30 years.

- **Thinking** — Write a financial plan. Run your own business. Plan the logical steps to solve a problem. Choose a job or career that requires a lot of technical knowledge. Watch TV and get annoyed with and criticize characters who can't hear you or get their feelings hurt. List the reasons someone needs to be hired or fired and how your team's effectiveness will be enhanced with either action.

- **Feeling** — Get with a friend and talk about your feelings. Do something good for someone else. Plan to be with people who have harmony, not controversy, as a goal. Enjoy harmony when you have it. Try to restore it when you don't without letting someone take advantage of you. Mentally put on a suit of armor like knights of old and deflect some negative feelings even if they are coming from family members.

- **Judging** — Be the one who makes decisions. You probably will not be happy unless you have the final say on some issues at work and at home. Be the boss who says the ultimate yes or no. Organize your closets, cabinets, drawers, garage. Give away clothes your children have outgrown, toys they don't play with, and clothes you haven't worn in six months. You choose the restaurant or movie. Plan your gym workouts for the next three months. Plan a vacation that is one to two years away.

- **Perceiving** — Gather information and let others make some of the decisions. Choose a job or career that lets you have some flexibility in deciding when projects get completed. Have an unscheduled Saturday when you do whatever occurs to you all day long. Read, write, garden, shop, paint, sew, knit, walk, hike, run — do all of them if time allows with no apologies for not sticking with anything long. Let someone else make the dinner plans.

Here's an example of a journal entry that shows my grabbing at what I need to restore myself:

> No one thing is the answer to returning to center, to slowing down enough and getting quiet enough to hear from God. No one thing solves all my discontent. But to be happy and productive again, I need quiet, I need exercise, I need to listen to my relaxation tape. I need to paint and write in my journal. I need an unstructured weekend. I need my husband in the wings to talk to when I'm ready, to go out to dinner with. I need life to be rocking along pretty well for my children, my mother. I am so blessed to have these things this weekend. Myers-Briggs helps me know what I need and helps me set the stage so I have the best chance of getting it.

When You Are in Trouble

The Myers-Briggs information helps you take care of yourself when life is fairly normal, but it can also give you clues about actions to take when you hit the rough spots. Think of the letters that are the opposite of your four preferred letters. Look at the list and decide which one you use the least. For me it is (T). I get into the most trouble if I overdo (F) behaviors and underdo (T). To get out of a mess, I often need to use Thinking to come up with a logical plan. I also use my (T) to help me be strong and get ready for the possibility that people may disapprove or be unhappy that I'm no longer going to work so hard to make everyone else happy.

Here are some examples of when I used my least preferred behavior (T) to help me solve problems at different stages of my life:

- **Young Children**

  When my children were driving me crazy fighting with each other, I would walk across the street to my neighbor's house and complain. (They were old enough to leave for a few minutes). She would let me wallow, whine, and cuss for several minutes and then make a suggestion. I would walk back in the kitchen door with a plan. The children would often take one look at me, sense the power was back, and instantly move away from each other.

- **Work**

  My organization has several big meetings a year. I used to teach day-long classes on Communication Skills at the meetings. Then, for health reasons, I could no longer do a 7-hour seminar in one day. To take care of myself, I had to set limits that others didn't always understand or like. I began to attend the meetings as a staff person rather than one of the faculty, but co-workers resented that I couldn't do the heavy lifting required to set up for a meeting. I came up with a plan to do career counseling during the meeting and bring in money that way.

- **Elderly parent**

  When I moved my mother from our family home in Virginia to a retirement community in Charlotte where I live, I had to have a plan to establish some equilibrium. At first I talked to her everyday, but I couldn't shake off her problems enough to do my job. After she had made many new friends and when her health was stable, we got into a good rhythm of a visit one week and a phone call the next. When I'm under a lot of pressure, she always tells me to take care of myself first. (I have been grateful that with her full-time teaching career, she often modeled that behavior when I was growing up.)

I rarely say negative things about those I love to others, but sometimes saying those things out loud to someone I trust and who I know won't throw it back in my face can help me get the strength to be tough when I go back and confront a difficult situation.

Here are behaviors you can use to solve a problem. As an experiment, just choose one — the behavior you use the least and decide if it would improve your situation.

E — Get out of the house and be with people.

I — Get by yourself, even if it is just a quick break in a bathroom stall to calm yourself.

S — Make a list of things to do in the order that would be most efficient.

N — Visualize the result you want to see happen.

T — Tell the whole truth even if it will hurt someone's feelings.

F — Tell less than the whole truth and spare someone's feelings.

J — Make that decision faster than you would want.

P — Delay making the decision as fast as you want to.

Choosing to do enough of your four preferred behaviors will boost your energy level. Experimenting with one of your least preferred behaviors can give you new solutions for solving a problem.

We can take any of our preferred behaviors and overuse them to the point that they do not serve us well. A book called *In the Grip* describes what happens when you go too far with a particular behavior. It has a list of suggestions for how to pull yourself out of stressful situations. It is a much more detailed description of the Myers-Briggs information. If you get it, start by reading about just your four letters so you are not overwhelmed. When people read the section on their letters, they often have the reaction — how did they know that about me? An example for me that was helpful: "Have time alone for as long as needed,"[26] I knew I needed to be alone to recover from overusing (F) behavior, but I felt guilty if I needed more than others thought reasonable.

Take the time you need to restore yourself. If your life circumstances don't immediately allow it, keep trying to change things until they do. For example, if you are an Introvert with small children, see if you can trade with someone to get a day alone and then keep their children later.

---

[26] Quenk, Naomi, *In the Grip*, p.18.

Influencing Others

Now lets talk about how the Myers-Briggs Type Indicator information can help you influence others. Problem solving and accomplishing goals may require trying to persuade others. That often calls for doing it "their way" not "our way."

When you want to communicate better with others and influence them, make a guess about one or two of their letters, then give them the kind of information they prefer and use their behavior style some of the time. This is a distilled summary of what I've found each letter wants. When I see people acting in the following ways, I make secret, educated guesses about their preferred behavior and then give them what I think they might want and see if it makes a difference.

- **E's** want to think through their ideas out loud. So let them talk, even ramble on until you find out what you need to know. If you are an Introvert, you also need to talk to them more than you might want to.

- **I's** want to think through ideas alone in quiet before they talk much about them. Don't rush an I. Describe your concept and then say, "Can we talk more about this tomorrow after you've had a chance to think about it?"

- **S's** want details and an orderly, step-by-step process. If you are shopping with an S, be thrilled that they will make a list of places you will go and the things you will look for in the order listed so you can make the best use of time.

- **N's** want to look at the future, the big picture and jump all over the place with ideas. If you are working with an N, be willing to start in the middle of a project and jump to another project if they suddenly have an idea about the second one. You can be the beneficiary of more of their creativity if you will not only let them do it, but respect them and not act as if they are scatter brained.

- **T's** like analysis and numbers. They want to say what they think and not have you get your feelings hurt — just listen to the logical reasons and think about cause and effect.

  An example of a T being logical and direct: "If you don't make the changes we asked for, we won't promote your product because we won't sell enough to make a profit." They would think and may add, "Don't take it personally."

- **F's** want harmony. They want people to be nice, not say hurtful things, and take turns talking. They also want to hear a personal story from you from time to time, ideally with some sharing of emotions. They also want a chance to tell you a personal story.

- J's want to decide quickly. They want you to make up your mind and do something soon even if it is wrong. They want to plan and schedule, bring structure and order.

- P's want to be flexible, go with the flow, not decide too quickly. They want to go shopping or on vacation and decide what to do next as they go along and not have it all planned out ahead of time. At work they would like to put off making decisions, even though most jobs require using a significant amount of J behavior for success.

The most flexible animals in nature last the longest. The most flexible human beings are often the most effective. People who understand their own preferences, make educated guesses about others' preferences, and give them information in their preferred style are the most influential.

Everyone has to use all the behaviors to keep a job. Be sure you get to do enough of your preferred behaviors at work or away from work to keep your energy level high.

If I do enough to honor my preferred behaviors (INFP), it is easier for me to change behaviors when needed. I can more easily perform the tasks of the opposite of my preferred letter when my work or personal life demands it: E — be with people, S — pay attention to details, T — let other people's problems not penetrate my soul, J — make decisions quickly.

If I take care of the needs of my first four preferred letters (INFP) at least on the weekends, I have energy to work the next week. I have enough love and compassion for myself that it overflows and I have some to give to others. If I take care of myself, then I feel connected, supported, and led by God — as if I am about what I was put here to do and be.

As Socrates said, it is important to know thyself. Realizing that self-knowledge is never complete or finished, I have found the Myers-Briggs Type Indicator a very useful tool for learning what I need to be happy and productive.

This chapter has been an introduction to MBTI. I recommend that you find someone to give the assessment to you with an explanation soon after you fill it out. The psychology department at your local university will most likely have a certified MBTI practitioner.

Works Cited

Kroeger, O., and J. Thuesen. *Type Talk*. New York, NY: Delacorte Press, 1988.

Kierkegaard, Soren. *Fear and Trembling and the Sickness Unto Death*, trans. and intro. and notes by Walter Lowrie. Princeton, New Jersey: Princeton University Press, 1974.

Laney, Marti Olsen. *The Introvert Advantage, How to Thrive in an Extravert World*. New York: Workman Publishing, 2002.

Myers, Isabel Briggs with Peter B. Myers. *Gifts Differing*. Palo Alto, CA: Consulting Psychologists Press, Inc., 1980.

Provost, Judith A. *Work, Play and Type*. Palo Alto, CA: Consulting Psychologists Press, Inc., 1990.

Quenk, Naomi L., *In the Grip*. Palo Alto, CA: CPP, Inc., 2000

Tieger, Paul D. & Barbara Barron-Tieger. *Do What You Are*. Boston: Little, Brown and Company, 1995.

Chapter 3

Plan What You Want

Eckhart Tolle and Oprah in their webcast to millions said we need to evolve from wanting something from the future or longing for the past to accepting and enjoying the present. While I agree with the concept, I think planning is necessary for a productive, satisfying life. The key is to plan for the future without getting too attached to it while accepting or enjoying every moment of the present as best you can.

You can get more of what you want if you do some planning, and, in this chapter, we'll look at a process for doing that. It's a self-coaching process that involves taking stock of your present, looking at your past, and then planning for the future.

Reflection can be beneficial. If you can look back over your life and see a pattern that makes some sense to you, you feel more secure, as if you are on the right track. The pattern gives you the courage to try new things, to take on the next challenge. Leland Kaiser, a health care futurist, has said that life can be viewed as an unfoldment process. This happened and then this happened. What would be the next unfoldment? What would be the next logical step that seems to grow out of the past?[27]

Richard Bolles of *What Color is Your Parachute* fame has described a study conducted on patients at a New York City hospital to see what made some patients heal faster than others after the same type of surgery. The researchers discovered that the fast healers were those who believed there was some meaning to everything that happened to them, even if that meaning was not evident at the time of the experience.[28]

---

[27] Barbara J Linney, MA. "Know Where You've Been Before You Decide Where to Go-Part 2," p.22.

[28] R. Bolles, *The Three Boxes of Life*, p. 354.

Such an attitude toward life is also helpful when you are not recovering from surgery, but are considering making changes in your life. Meaning is a word with a slippery definition. It's an individual concept. My meaning will be different from yours, and that's fine. It's just important that we both find some.

Often meaning becomes clearer quite a while after the event. I had made a weekly drive to another city that seemed a waste of time and money. I could not make sense of it, but after a couple of years I could look back and impose meaning on it that made me feel better. After I moved to Florida in 1983, I decided to work on a PhD in English in Tampa. I lived in Orlando, so that meant driving 100 miles each way every week, spending 1-2 nights away from my family. I did the trek for three years. In the last course in the summer session, I turned in my proposal for my PhD dissertation to the professor whose class I had been in all summer. I had been working on the proposal all through his class and received regular feedback from him about it. When I turned it in the last night, he said, "I hope you will do this study sometime." I said, "Sometime? We have been talking about this being my dissertation proposal." He said, "Well, I don't know if a committee will approve it." I walked out thinking, "how much longer can I jump through academic hoops?"

At the same time, I landed my first consulting job with the American Management Association to teach a 4-day course on business writing. My consulting career took off once I had worked for AMA because they were very respected in the profession. For several years I thought, "Why did I drive to Tampa for three years taking courses?" At first it seemed so futile since I wasn't going to finish, but later a different answer occurred to me — so I could learn to spend the night alone in a hotel and not be afraid. I do that all the time now and relish the solitude. Yet the first time I did it, I spent the night reading the Gideon Bible and praying for courage. (Young women may have a hard time imagining fear of being alone in a hotel, but many women of my generation went from their family's home to their husband's home with no alone time in between.)

Several months later I took a job with an organization in Tampa — an unexpected and marvelous career move for me. I didn't have to move there. I had a home office in Orlando that was connected to them by computer, phone and fax, and I went to the Tampa office once a month.

I didn't get what I thought I wanted when I started working on the PhD — to be a tenured professor in a college teaching English. But while working toward it, I got something else that I wanted more, a wonderful career as the Vice President of Career Development at the American College of Physician Executives. When I am thrown off course or become unsettled, I am comforted when I remember the unexpected events in the past that eventually turned out well.

The Howards in *Exploring the Road Less Traveled* said,

> "Most of us learn best, really learn, from our own experience – not simply from having things happen to us but from reflecting on what happens, both alone and in exchanges with others, so that the meaning of our experience becomes clear and we can make choices based on growing awareness rather than unchallenged assumptions."[29]

A good way to find meaning and get more of what you want in life is to take stock of the present, look back at the past, and then plan for the future. All three steps benefit from writing. The first exercise is called the "Now Moment Questions," the second is "Steppingstones," and the third is "Planning Your Future."

Taking Stock of the Present

The following exercise called "Now Moment Questions" is adapted from an exercise done by Ira Progoff in an "At a Journal Workshop."[30] The questions will help you take stock of the present. I do them every 3-4 months and the answers are different every time although some of the themes will stay the same.

I use these questions when I begin career counseling with my clients. My daughter and other members of her firm use them to begin coaching relationships. We have found that they benefit all personality types.

Instructions for How to Answer the Questions

Answer the questions by using the same freewriting style that I described in Chapter 1. Write without worrying about spelling, punctuation, grammar, or anything someone told you to worry about. My mother once said to me, "Don't put in writing anything you wouldn't be willing to see on the front page of the newspaper the next morning." The message stuck, and I had to get that voice out of my head to write what I was really thinking and feeling. I did it by promising myself I would destroy anything that no one should see.

---

29 Howard, and Howard, *Exploring the Road Less Traveled*, p.10.

30 Nelson, "Learning From Within: Ira Progoff and the Power of Personal Writing," p.66.

However, there is one catch. Start writing and don't stop for two minutes whether or not you can think of anything in answer to the question that I have asked. You can write longer than two minutes on each question if you want to but not less. If writing by hand is tough because you don't do it much, try resting in between the questions.

Get a timer. Set aside at least 30 minutes of quiet time and answer the following ten questions. Write two minutes on each of the questions. If you can't think of anything to write, just start writing anyway and keep writing — "I can't think of anything" over and over. There is a reason for this — ideas will occur to you if you keep writing that will not occur if you just sit and think.

1. Write one thing you like about your present job. (outside the home or at home)

2. Write one thing that frustrates you about your job. (outside the home or at home)

3. What kinds of things are you putting your energy into now? (Either at work or away from work)

4. What kinds of things are you struggling with?

5. If you had a magic genie, what would you command it to do to solve one of your problems?

6. Who are the people who are important to you? List them and write a few things about them.

7. What are your dreams and hopes?

8. Name an image or a picture that describes your life right now. For example: My life is like a roller coaster — up one minute and down the next. Or, my life is like banana pudding — it tastes good but I am drowning in it. Or, my life is like a field of flowers — I am so excited about picking a bouquet. (If this is hard for you, just write over and over — What is my life like? What is my life like? And see if any image comes to you. Sometimes it does and sometimes it doesn't.)

9. Is there something you would like to get from this writing exercise today? Sometimes the answer is "no." That's fine. Just keep writing about anything for two minutes.

10. List some things you do to take care of yourself.

A word of caution – writing will often take you places you didn't know you were going to go. Be careful with the words you generate. If you write something very risky and no one should ever see it, then tear it up when you finish. You do not have to keep it to benefit from having written it. **Do not do this exercise on your computer at work or in an email system.**

The following is an example of some of the answers I wrote on one occasion:

1. **Write one thing you like about your present job.** (outside the home or at home) I like that I work alone in my home office during the week and write and paint in that office on the weekends. Travel and teach programs around the country. What else? What else? Work with creative people and some who are very cooperative, some not so much.

2. **Write one thing that frustrates you about your job.** (outside the home or at home) The unending stream of emails that demand to be answered, that hang over me and the fear that I will miss something important. When I get back from vacation, there can be several hundred there. Sometimes I fall into a trap of mentally cracking a whip and yelling go faster, faster. If I forget to stand up and walk around periodically, I can freeze my back into a painful position that may take days of rest and my acupuncturist to fix.

3. **What kinds of things are you putting your energy into now?** (either at work or away from work) Praying for my children's happiness. Work which is going well. Painting. Visiting my mother who lives in a retirement community here. Helping my 12 year old cocker spaniel who has lost his eyesight. Doing things that will eliminate back stiffness. Got new mattress and box springs. Mattresses are huge now. Felt so high up the first 2 or 3 nights. Got new office chair for computer. Looking for chair and ottoman where I can sit when listening to conference calls. I need to walk around or change sitting locations every hour.

4. **What kinds of things are you struggling with?** Not worrying excessively. If I don't control my mind, I dream up all kinds of bad things that could happen. Every misfortune I read or hear about I think – "that could happen to me or a loved one." I need to renew and cultivate my own friends rather than putting so much energy into worrying about family members.

5. **If you had a magic genie, what would you command it to do to solve one of your problems?** Good words would flow effortlessly to me. I would finish this book

without struggling. The words would continue to bring comfort to me. It would get published and bring comfort to others. I'd wave a magic wand and give my children what they want. Concentrate on your own life not theirs. Who am I trying to kid? I'll always be thinking about theirs.

6. **Who are the people who are important to you? List them and write a few things about them.** Husband, daughter, son, daughter-in-law, grandchildren, mother, other family members and a few friends. We celebrated our anniversary. We live happily and comfortably together. I have an office on the first floor of my home and my husband has his office on the second floor. I am so grateful he is in my life.

7. **What are your dreams and hopes?** Good health for everyone. Children successful, getting the loved ones and work they want. All of us serving you oh God. Have money for secure retirement in this house as long as we can stay here and then money to pay for retirement community when necessary. Would like to have enough money to give to children when I choose without it being harmful to them in some way. Write always, even if it is just for myself. Let writing be my old-age exercise to keep my mind alert the way some people play bridge, do cross word puzzles or Sudoku.

8. **Name an image or a picture that describes your life right now.** The waterfalls at Linville. We have been a sturdy rock base through which these children have come. Let them go, let them flow through. I am trying to do that and I am painting a picture of Linville Falls to hang in my office to remind me to let go.

9. **Is there something you would like to get from this writing exercise today?** World peace, inner peace, the next thing I want to do for play, the next thing I want to do for work.

10. **List some things you do to take care of yourself.** Walk, eat nourishing food, get enough sleep, listen to relaxation tape. Read, write, paint, sew, knit, dance.

When I actually do these questions, they have more whining in them than I have shown here. I didn't think you'd want to read over and over — I'm hungry, I still miss having a cup of tea in the morning after years of being off caffeine, can't think of anything, keep writing till you finish 2 minutes, keep writing, keep writing, etc. Just know some of that will be peppered throughout what you write.

My daughter added these reflection questions when she started using them with her clients:

"Once you have finished writing answers to the Now Moment questions, the following questions may help you to reflect and find meaning.

1. Did you gain any insight?

2. Did you see any patterns?

3. Did anything surprise you?

4. Did anything please you?

5. Did anything concern you?

6. Can you identify any action you should take?

While these reflection questions can often be helpful, you may also find that you benefit from simply answering the Now Moment questions and waiting for insight at a later time."[31]

The "Now Moment" questions above help you figure out what is going on right now — what problems are bothering you, whether you are deliriously happy vacationing in the mountains, what important people are on your radar screen this month, and what your short- and long-term dreams are.

Let the "Now Moment" questions settle in your system for several days or weeks before you do the next exercise. When you feel ready for a next step, take a look backward at what has brought you to where you are today and see if you see some patterns emerge.

Looking At the Past

After you have thought about your life in the present, you need to look back and see what events brought you to this point. "Those who cannot remember the past are condemned to repeat it." These words of George Santayana's are as true for individuals as they are for nations. This "looking at the past" exercise, recommended by Ira Progoff, involves listing the "Steppingstones" of your life — the significant events that have led you to where you are today.[32] Don't feel this has to be a definitive list in correct order. Just write the items quickly and effortlessly as they occur to you.

Here is one of my "Steppingstones" lists from a particular day. (Other times they are very different — once I listed all the men and boys I have loved.) Don't let my list constrict you. Let yours be whatever pops into your head.

---

[31] Allison Partners, LLC, 2004.

[32] I. Progoff, *At a Journal Workshop*, pg. 10.

- Born — lived first 10 years in Port Royal, Virginia — where US 301 and 17 intersect.

- Moved to Fredericksburg — big city (about 20,000) 20 miles from Port Royal.

- Graduated from James Monroe — thought it was the best high school in the area. Felt so fortunate to have moved from a cross-roads town to a city school.

- Westhampton College — women's division of the University of Richmond. Dated at the University of Virginia on the weekends.

- Tapped Mortar Board president. There were only 10 of us. Our parents were in the audience unbeknownst to us. I was the last one called because I was going to be president. Right when I thought I didn't have a chance, I heard my Daddy's distinctive cough. My heart leapt up.

- Married Charlie after 3 years of dating.

- Divorced after 2 years of marriage. Heart broken, heart sick — thought all my dreams had ended.

- Married George after 6 months of dating.

- Lived one year in Charlottesville, VA, with George before we moved — had lived there 2 years with Charlie. Loved Charlottesville even when I was unhappy with Charlie.

- Moved to Charlotte, NC.

- Had daughter, Allison.

- Had son, George.

- Taught in the youth department of Myers Park Baptist Church — they trained their teachers by sending them to a personal growth lab, teaching them small group dynamics and design skills.

- Started graduate school — had tried golf, symphony women's auxiliary, medical auxiliary — nothing satisfied me until I audited a course in the religion department.

- Got MA in English from UNCC.

- Moved to Orlando — children were 8 and 10.

- Depressed — left good teaching job, friends, and church so husband could make a good career move for him.

- Did 15-week CHAANGE program that ended panic attacks.[33]

- Started work on a PhD in English.

- Taught Business Writing for the American Management Association.

- Went to work for American College of Physician Executives.

- Wrote book, *Hope for the Future: A Career Development Guide for Physician Executives.*

- Taught Communication Skills in Physician in Management course.

- Had 2 surgeries.

- Now teach courses, do Career counseling, and write – wonderful combination.

After you have made your list, think about the following questions:

1. What do you wish you had not done?

2. What do you wish you had done?

3. Do you see some meaning or a pattern that makes sense to you?

4. Do you see a natural progression?

An example of how I answered these questions and then how a client answered them follows:

My Answers:

1. **What do you wish you had not done?** Wish I had not lifted that suitcase with too many clothes in it 8 months after my first surgery.

2. **What do you wish you had done?** Said to my boss that I wanted to teach 3½ hours instead of 7. David Whyte said – do what you are called to do and do it in a way that is right for you. You can be doing the right thing but in a way that will kill you. That is what a 7-hour speaking day was doing to me, but 3½ hours is fine

3. **Do you see some meaning or a pattern that makes sense to you?** I have always loved Charlottesville. When I was 20 years old, my daddy said when we came over the crest of the hill on 250 West, my face lit up. It would seem right for my daughter to own property here. She can rent it if she leaves. I have an ongoing commitment to finding the balance of supporting my grown children and yet letting them live their own

---

33 More information about this in Chapter 7.

lives. I have learned I have given too much when I secretly feel I have a right to tell them what to do.

4. **Do you see a natural progression or something you could learn from the past?** A natural progression might be to help her buy a house in Charlottesville.

Here are the answers to the same questions from one of my coaching clients:

1. **What do you wish you had not done?** "Wish I had not divorced my first wife. In my third marriage, I'm still dealing with the same problems. I might as well have stayed in the first one and worked the problems out. It certainly would have been better for my children and probably better for me."

2. **What do you wish you had done?** "I wish I had become a history professor instead of going to medical school."

3. **Do you see some meaning or a pattern that makes sense to you?** "When I look at the past, I see a pattern of leaving situations quickly when they became difficult (a marriage, 3 jobs). I don't want to do that in this current crisis. I want to take time to think, move slower, sit with the pain a little longer, and perhaps make a better decision than some I've made in the past."

4. **Do you see a natural progression or something you could learn from the past?** "Don't leave job yet. I want to stay longer than I have in the past when things got tough and see if I can work through the difficulties."

Often we live life at breakneck speed, without stopping to see what we can learn from what we have done. It is often scary to slow down and process information, but the rewards can be great if you can sit with the uneasiness a little while. Progoff claims that to think about "the past periods of our lives gives us access to the unlived possibilities of our existence which the future may still give us an opportunity to fulfill, albeit in a different form."[34]

Planning Your Future

After you have reflected on the present in the "Now Moments" and the past in the "Steppingstones," you are ready to set some goals for your future. Let your imagination run wild. List all of the things you want in your professional and private life.

---

[34] I. Progoff, *At a Journal Workshop*, p.262.

When you make the list, you may think all sorts of strange messages or hear voices from the past such as: "I don't deserve it. I never really wanted it anyway. What about the starving, dying people who can't have what they want? You are getting too big for your britches. You are getting above your raising. Who do you think you are?" Either ignore or write the thoughts down, but keep on making the list. Try to overcome the forces of resistance that keep you from thinking about what you really want in life. Write anything you desire, even if it is unreasonable, because no one else will know about it unless you choose for them to know.

Martha Beck in *The Joy Diet* wrote, "I can tell you from extensive observation that refusing to feel desire is the only thing more painful than failing to get what you want, and that learning not to yearn, far from preventing disappointment, ultimately guarantees it."[35]

Example of a List of Wants

- Good health.

- Work for me and my husband

- Continue living with him in this house and be able to take good care of the house.

- Continue my job.

- Children to have what they want in career and family.

- Mother to be healthy.

- All of us to be serving God and our neighbors.

- Church and our minister to do well.

- Finish this book and write others.

If you have trouble making a "Want List" start by making a list of things you don't want. That can often break the logjam. After enough negatives have poured out on the page, you can begin to list what you do want.

Example of Things I Didn't Want To Do

- I took a babysitter with us on vacation when my children were 6 months and 3 years old. Everyone else was doing it. I hated having an extra person with us.

---

35 Beck, *The Joy Diet: 10 Daily Practices for a Happier Life*, p.49.

- As unmotherly as it sounds, I did not like family vacations where all four of us had to be in a car to get there. That was too many high-energy people in a small space for this Introvert. Kids would fight. Husband would play loud music. My body felt racked by the penetrating noise. The longer the trip the more jumpy I became. Now that the children are grown and it is just the two of us in a car, it is better, but I still don't like music not of my choosing or the sound of ball games or the cars rushing toward us or the way my body feels after two hours in the car.

I have done many things one time or several times, but when I figured out I didn't like them, I stopped doing them.

After you have made an exhaustive list of things you want, holding back nothing, pick one that you would like to think more about. Answer the following questions:

1. What do you want?

2. What will you have to pay (sacrifice) to get it?

3. What might be an obstacle to getting what you want?

4. Picture yourself already having it. What do you see?

5. What is one thing you could do each day that moves you toward your goal?

Example:

1. **What do you want?** Heal pulled muscles

2. **What will you have to pay (sacrifice) to get it?** Rest

3. **What might be an obstacle to getting what you want?** The things I think of to do to keep me busy.

4. **Picture yourself already having it**. I see myself strong, healthy and making presentations with energy and enthusiasm.

5. **What one thing can you do each day that moves you toward your goal?** Be quiet, do mental work not physical work until the muscles are healed.

Now make a list of the top 3-5 desires you want to keep in mind. You can answer the above five questions for each one or not. Put these goals where you can see them. Glance at them, but don't become obsessed or overly worried about them. The seeds have been planted. They may flower in a month or years down the road.

Now go about your daily business without too much concern. Do a little each day or each week that is related to your goals. The authors of *Life by Design* write:

> *"Planning is like driving in a fog. You can see only a short distance in front of you, which means you have to go slowly at first. Every time you move forward, more of the road is revealed. At some point the fog clears and you can speed up. All plans, from changing a career to breaking a habit, to writing a book, to rearing your children with self-esteem, are made up of such small steps. Though you may not know all the steps right now, it is essential that you write down what you do know and begin to move forward. Let it be OK to not know."*[36]

Once I wrote down some things I wanted and forgot about them. I came across the list several years later. I was amazed and pleased to find that I was doing three out of the five items. Here is an example of one of them:

Three years before I lived in it, I drew a picture of my ideal house in a creativity workshop — two-story brick with living room and dining room on one side, an office on the other, a kitchen and den behind the office. I thought no one would build a floor plan like that. I wanted almost no grass to cut.

At the time I had no plans to change houses, much less cities. Three years later we had an opportunity to move back to Charlotte. On a two-day house-hunting trip, we looked at about ten houses and put a bid in on one.

On the plane ride home from the two-day, house-hunting trip, I remembered the workshop I'd gone to three years earlier. I went home, scrounged through a closet, found the journal and was amazed at how close my drawing was to the house we were trying to buy. It was even on a pie-slice shaped lot with grass in the front yard that can be cut in 15 minutes. The back yard (the wide part of the pie slice) was all trees with no grass.

I had not been thinking about it or even remembering the desire during those three years. The opportunity to move and buy a new house came up suddenly and unexpectedly. My husband and I now live in that house and work out of home offices. His is on the second floor, mine is on the first, each with separate heating and air conditioning units — an important feature since he works best in a warm room and I in a cool one. I am grateful every day.

---

[36] Kirschner and Brinkman, *Life by Design: Making Wise Choices in a Mixed-Up World*, p.56.

Self Coaching

This three-step process of examining the present, past and future is a way to coach your-self. I do it about every six months or more if I'm feeling overwhelmed or confused. Then I write about what I discover for several days afterward in my daily, 15 minute, freewriting sessions.

Here's an example of action steps I came up with in freewriting several days after I had done the "Now Moment" questions, "Steppingstones," and making my Want List:

- Renew and cultivate my own life and friends — do less thinking about my grown children's lives.

- Design workshop on improving physician/nurse relationships.

- Continue working on my own personal book.

- Rewrite career book for work.

I have used this process repeatedly for myself and for clients for more than 20 years. It has helped me figure out what I am worried about, why, and what I can do about it. It has done the same for those I have coached.

Hire a Coach or Counselor

If I can't find enough peace and direction on my own, I pay a coach or counselor. Some view this as a character flaw. I don't. I think it is a chance with someone's else's perspective to see if your life needs some mid-course adjustments. I started when my children were five and two. When they were teenagers, I went once a month — I needed someone objective to listen to what was going on and give me a suggestion of something new to try. I have gone about every five years since. My husband, a pediatrician, used to talk about the importance of yearly "well-baby" checkups. Talking things over with a counselor or coach is a "well-psyche" check up.

The Unexpected and Unwanted

Sometimes you don't get what you want, but you get something else that might be better in the long run. Unexpected and unwanted developments can have an impact on your future in ways you can't imagine. As a senior in high school, I was in charge of the home-coming decorations. I decided to cover the inner tube of huge tractor tire with broken mirror pieces and hang it in the middle of the gym. It would sparkle like the rotating balls that were later popular during the disco period in the '80s. I had a steady stream of people coming into my house all hours of the night and day, going to the basement, gluing on broken mirror pieces.

When it was finished, I went upstairs, exhausted, to get ready for bed and saw red spots all over my stomach. My mother said, "You have the measles." I had that awful feeling that I could not miss school and yet realized the gig was up. I settled into two weeks of absolute misery with a throat so sore I kept my head under the bedspread so I wouldn't breath room temperature air and the light wouldn't hurt my eyes. In the dark with the covers over my head, my mother slowly read to me over and over Wordsworth and Coleridge, my senior English class assignments.

Some lines penetrated my soul. Coleridge's "Water, water, everywhere, and not a drop to drink." Wordsworth's "The child is the father of the man... We come trailing clouds of glory." It was the first time I understood poetry. Later in college it gave me the courage to major in English, eventually become an English professor, and much later a consultant teaching communication skills. When I was raising children, Wordsworth's lines would go through my head and I'd think — they have come from God. They will give me mes-sages and teach me things. They did and still do.

At the time when I had the measles, I thought going to the homecoming dance was the most important thing in the world, but it turned out that listening to poetry read in the dark would positively influence my life for years to come.

I know some of you are thinking — there is no way I'm getting anything I want in my situation. None of us gets out of life alive, so eventually we hit the wall with wanting, but there is a great deal of living to do in the mean time. So want, plan, achieve and live life well. We can ask God to help us now and when the time comes for our death and whatever goes with getting ready for it, to help us be brave and faithful as we cross over to the other side to be with her/him.

We have to live with the paradox of wanting and delaying gratification. However, as Bolles says, "You have got to know what it is you want, or someone is going to sell you a bill of goods somewhere along the line that can do irreparable damage to your self-esteem, your sense of worth, and your stewardship of the talents God gave you."[37]

---

37 R. Bolles, *The Three Boxes of Life*, p.82.

Want what you want, and then expect to work to get it. Give yourself permission to make the list. Then pull back and be happy with what you have while working toward what you want. As Eckhart Tolle wrote in the *The New Earth*, "Even though you have a goal, what you are doing in the present moment needs to remain the focal point of your attention; otherwise, you will fall out of alignment with universal purpose."[38]

If you can stand the tension of wanting yet happily waiting and working, you'll get more of what you want than those who never stretch themselves to think about it. Without goals, you stagnate and go backward. With goals, you are drawn toward exciting possibilities. If you run out of things to strive for, you lose your zest for living.

Works Cited

Beck, Martha. *The Joy Diet: 10 Daily Practices for a Happier Life*. New York: Crown Publishers, 2003.

Bolles, R. *The Three Boxes of Life*. Berkeley, CA: Ten Speed Press, 1981.

Howard, W. and Howard, A. *Exploring the Road Less Traveled: A Study Guide for Small Groups*. New York: Simon & Schuster, 1985.

Kirschner, Dr. Rick and Dr. Rick Brinkman. *Life by Design: Making Wise Choices in a Mixed-Up World*. New York: McGraw-Hill, 1999.

Linney, Allison. "Reflection Questions." Charlottesville, VA: Allison Partners, LLC, 2009.

Linney, Barbara J., MA. "Know Where You've Been Before You Decide Where to Go — Part 2," *Physician Executive*, Sept-Oct, Vol. 17, Issue 5, pp22-25.

Nelson, Lynn G. "Learning From Within: Ira Progoff and the Power of Personal Writing," *Media and Methods*. September 1978, p.112 in Barbara Linney, MA. *The Chosen Self Dances in a Writing Class*. MA Thesis for University of North Carolina at Charlotte, 1982.

Progoff, I. *At a Journal Workshop*. New York, NY: Simon and Schuster, 1985.

Tolle, Eckhart. *A New Earth: Awakening to Your Life's Purpose*. London: A Plume Book, 2005.

---

[38] E. Tolle, *The New Earth*, p.304.

Chapter 4

Listen When You Care

Listening is an important skill you can develop to get what you want out of life. Listening helps people heal from whatever blows life has dealt them. All of us hunger to be heard. We want at least one person to know who we really are and love us anyway. This can only happen if that someone is willing to listen to us. If you listen closely with caring and without judgment, you give a life-changing gift.

While it is truly a gift to others to listen well, it can often also get you what you want — others will listen to you and they are more likely to take the action you want them to take.

I can tell you how to listen, but I can't make you want to, and wanting to is absolutely essential to doing it. I'll describe four life situations that motivated me to develop and then fine-tune the skill.

My grandmother

I listen out of interest but also out of fear. I am often trying to find the safe spot in my environment. When I was little, if I listened to my father, mother, brother, grandmother, I thought I could figure out how to make enough of them happy that the tension would leave the house. My father's mother lived with my parents for 18 years. I was alive for the last 10. She was a complaining, negative person who resented that my mother had married her baby. The tension in the house was palpable, and I cared about that and disliked it for as long as I can remember. I could feel the tension in my body long before I had any words to understand or try to fix it. So I listened intently. My mother cared. From my child's viewpoint, my father did not seem to care because he was the other half of the arguments. I cared too much.

My father

When my brother became a teenager who rebelled, he and my father argued. He was 16; I was 14. I wanted peace so I listened for ways I could make it happen. Since most of the time my father adored me, I thought I had a favored-child status and could influence him. I took it upon myself to explain to him that he wasn't treating my brother fairly. He said, "I'll fix it so you and your mother don't have to put up with me." He stormed out of the house. I was terrified thinking he meant divorce or suicide. I went to my mother and told her what I had done. She said, "Don't worry about it. He will get over it." And he did, but he barely spoke to me for a week and then he was back to his jovial self without any explanation. It took me a lot longer to get over it.

Most of the time, I received great love and support from my father as you will see in the next example. Since I have raised my own children, I feel guilty that this one incident loomed large and became so important in my head especially since I can point to instances when I screwed up big time as a parent. However, I tell it because it was a watershed incident in the development of my communication skills, especially with men. I have had to learn to say what I want from men and not worry about what they were going to do to themselves or care that they were giving me the silent treatment. My father gave me the first chance to try it. It didn't go well with him, but I have improved my technique, become braver as an adult, and gotten good results.

My divorce

I've also been listened to. I married the first time as soon as I graduated from college. Two years later my husband walked out at 4:30 in the morning. At 6:30am I called home. My father answered the phone. I cried hysterically. He said, "Can you go to work?" I said, "Yes, I can't stand to stay home alone." He said, "I don't know what I'll do, but I'll do something." When I arrived at my teaching job at 7:30am, I called my mother at her teaching job. She said, "Daddy is on his way." He drove ten hours to Nashville.

My father was an Extravert and <u>always</u> said what he thought — this time he didn't. I cried and told the story until the tears ran out. Then he took me out to eat. I couldn't eat. He said, "Take a little bite of food, a little sip of water, and chew slowly, then swallow." As soon as I ate, the tears would begin again. For 48 hours he listened and did not give advice. I finally said, "I feel like every decision I have made for the last five years has been wrong. I'm going to make one more that may be wrong. I'm going home."

My father gained a lifetime of redemption by listening for two days and not telling me what to do. He waited until I worked it out. Then he went to the phone, called my mother and said, "Come out here. She's coming home. I need some help."

She came, they packed, and we left.

My children — Room Time and Time Together

I had to learn to listen in a new way when I had young children. I talked to my minister who recommended a counselor who practiced in a two-story brick building called Children's House.

I went to the counselor when my daughter was five because she screamed at me a lot, and, too often, I screamed back. She wanted every minute of my time all day long, and increasingly I didn't want to give her any because she whined, begged, screamed, and was never satisfied. She could feel that I didn't want to be with her and that made her crave me more.

My parents hinted that I should just give her a good spanking. That would shape her up as it had my brother when he threw a tantrum in Woolworths 30 years before. I had tried that. It didn't work, and, frankly, I spanked too hard.

I thought the counselor would listen to the story of my daughter's unrelenting demands and tell me to bring her in so she could fix her. The counselor said, "No, I think just you and I need to talk." My pride was hurt. I wanted to be thought of as a good mother even though right then I would have liked to quit the job.

The counselor said, "You are the only one who has a chance of being in control of the screaming. She is too young." So we came up with a plan.

Part One of the plan was when she had a screaming fit, she had to stay in her room until she could calm down. A child's gate was put in her doorway. The first time I put her in there, I sat half way down the steps so she couldn't see me. I cried and prayed for this plan to work.

Every ten minutes I was to go to her and calmly say, "I'm fine. As soon as you can stop crying, you can come out." After a long time, she said, "I am stoppin' cryin' mama," with great sobs between the words. The minute she stopped I went to her. We had to do this frequently in the beginning, but a new process was in place for both of us. It was the beginning of a new, wonderful relationship and my pulling out of my depression of raising very young children.

Part Two of the plan was that I was to spend an hour a day with her doing whatever she wanted and listening closely as long as she didn't scream at me. If she did, then we would stop and I'd say, "Well, we will try again tomorrow during 'time together.'" We could sit side by side and color with crayons or markers in a coloring book. If she suddenly decided she wanted to finish the picture I was coloring instead of hers, I let her. We could play a game where she made up the rules. It was an "ah ha" for me: that I didn't have to teach her the correct way to play the game. I thought I had some cosmic parental obligation to make her do it right. (When she read this, she said, "I still need to make up my own rules. I didn't remember you let me start that early.")

We could not shop — it was hectic and she did not get my undivided attention so the hunger to be heard was not fed. We could not bake cookies although I thought all mothers and daughters should do that. I would yell before it was over when the flour landed on the ceiling or the floor.

Part Three of the plan was that she would spend an hour alone in her room entertaining herself. It was hard at first, but soon she learned to enjoy it. She is an Extravert, but as a grown woman, she says required "room time" is the reason she can enjoy being alone and restoring herself after much outward activity. She has also said it helps her honor the needs of the Introverts in her life.

I tell you these stories to help you remember your own stories about why you listen or why you don't. Listening is a well-ingrained habit in me developed over years from my need to restore harmony wherever I am. I learned this skill through some tough times and through good times, and it has served my personal and professional life well.

My father was loving many more times than he was hurtful. Both parents listened carefully when I talked. My mother listened seldom passing judgment. My father always told his opinion, but he did listen. No matter how well our parents did most of the time, I think we zero in on their mistakes and shape our lives in response to them. Before I had children, I was either frightened or angry about the times my parents didn't get it right. After I had children and started making my own mistakes, I rationalized it was God's way of making us all turn to him/her for help.

Reasons for Listening

We have many reasons for listening. My daughter is a great, compassionate listener, but she will tell you that before she developed an appreciation of listening, she sometimes needed to find another reason to exert the energy it takes to listen well. In the early days of her career, she found she could get people to do what she wanted them to do if she listened to them. At first she thought telling them over and over to do it would get the job done, but then she learned listening to their concerns was much more effective. In Myers-Briggs terms she is a Thinking type and being effective matters most to her. My husband says he listens because he wants people to like him. He is a Feeling type so being liked is a strong motivator to him.

What are your reasons? To be safe? To be liked? To get people to do what you want them to do? To get information you need? To learn? Think about your most secret needs that can motivate you to listen. Most of what we do can be traced to what can seem a selfish desire. Even helping others makes us feel good. Try to get ok with that and hunt for what drives you to listen or what keeps you from it. I can promise you this — if people in your life feel heard, they won't care why you listened. They will appreciate that you took the time.

How to Listen

Listening is an art that starts with attentive silence. It is hard work. Swets describes why listening is so difficult:

> *"While an average speech rate for many people is about 200 words per minute, most of us can think about four times that speed. With all that extra think time, the ineffective listener lets his mind wander. His brain takes excursions to review the events of yesterday, or plan tomorrow, or solve a business problem...or sleep."*[39]

You have to work to take control of your mind and make it concentrate on what is being said. If you are troubled by an impending law suit, a divorce, or a child who is having problems, your capacity to listen will diminish drastically. You will need to be patient with yourself and perhaps tell the person, "I am a bit distracted; can you tell me that again?" or "I find I'm not able to concentrate, and I really want to listen to you. Could we reschedule?"

The listening process cannot be exactly prescribed, but there are techniques that will help you become better at it.

- Be quiet. If you are interrupting often, you have not yet begun to listen. Stop talking, look interested, choose a good place with no distracting background noise. Concentrate. Try to calm the internal chatter that goes on in your head. Stop whatever you are doing.

---

[39] Swets, *The Art of Talking So That People Will Listen*, p.42.

- Use your body to let the person know you are there. Lying on the sofa watching TV, reading the newspaper at the breakfast table, folding laundry, opening mail or reading email in your office while someone talks to you are not good positions for listening. You may think you can do both things at the same time, but the talker does not think so. If it is an important conversation, you must stop what you are doing and turn your face and body toward the speaker.

As mentioned in the introduction, when my daughter was little, she started to talk later than most of her playmates, but once she started talking, she didn't stop. I remember preparing dinner while she was talking and she came up to me, tugged at my skirt and said, "Mama, turn your face." She knew I had to stop what I was doing and look at her and be quiet to listen the way she wanted to be heard.

When I visit my mother in her retirement community, we sit at the small round table I painted to go in her apartment. We eat dinner – just the two of us, look in each other's eyes, and I believe she feels heard. At first we went to the main dining room. If someone joined us for dinner, I might as well not have gone because we could not connect, and I could not give her my undivided attention.

Rick Pitino in *Success is a Choice* wrote:

> "The art of listening is looking at someone when he or she speaks to you, not over his or her shoulder at who else might be in the room. It's hearing what the person is saying to you instead of thinking about what you're going to say next. It's making eye contact, which not only is courteous but gives the person with whom you're speaking the sense that you truly care what he or she is saying to you. Making eye contact develops trust."[40]

- Strive to make eye contact 80% of the time.[41] Don't turn it into a staring contest. It's natural to look away and think for a little, but turn back soon.

- Give an occasional "uh huh" or head nod. It helps the talker get the message out. Kirschner and Brinkman demonstrate the point in their book *Life by Design*:

> "Give people feedback that you're listening, whether it's a nod of the head, a meaningful look, or an occasional grunt. Do you know why people repeat themselves? Do you know why? Do you? People repeat themselves because they want feedback that they've been heard."[42]

---

40 Pitino, *Success is a Choice*, p.133

41 This chapter on listening is written primarily for successful communication in the United States. If you are working with people from cultures other than your own, you must commit to learning effective listening skills for those situations. How we do it may vary, but I'm pretty sure wanting to be heard is a universal human desire.

42 Kirschner, Dr. Rick and Dr. Rick Brinkman, *Life by Design: Making Wise Choices in a Mixed-Up World*, p.203.

However, don't over do it. Too much head nodding makes you look like a bobble-head doll. It is often misinterpreted and can send the message that you are subordinate. Women are more often guilty of over doing head nodding. The woman is usually indicating that she is listening, but the man may think she is agreeing with everything he says.

I had a friend who constantly said "uh huh" when I was talking to her. Instead of helping me get the words out, I felt every "uh huh" was — "Shut up, shut up, shut up and let me talk."

• When listening, make your face soft, stern, or neutral whichever is appropriate, but not stone-faced, bored, or frowning. Look in the mirror and practice. You can soften your face by smiling ever so slightly. A stone-faced or bored look is no effort at all to control the muscles in your face — can even be slack jawed. Do not let your eyes wander. No smirking.

• Ask non-judgmental questions. Deborah Tannen wrote in *That's Not What I Meant*:

> "Questions, like sarcasm, are favorite forms of criticism precisely because they are indirect — like shots from a gun with a silencer. The wounded feels the effect, swift and sure, but the source of the attack is hard to locate."[43]

Questions can sound innocent, but in fact, can be cruel.

My father was very intuitive and could zero in on the heart of a problem with a pointed question. When I was going through stressful times, I could hold myself together as an adult if he didn't ask me too many questions. I have the same penetrating question skill he did. It is a very useful trait in my career counseling work, but it can be too intrusive with family members if I am not careful.

Don't ask, "Why did you do that?" There is no decent answer to that question. When you ask, you are implying that the person was the village idiot for doing it. You may be absolutely right, but if you want the conversation to continue, you are going to have to resist saying all that you know. Here are some examples of non-judgmental questions that help the conversation progress — What do you think you'll do next? When will you let them know your decision? Would it be useful if I helped you think of some additional options?

Ask questions sparingly and don't use them as a secret way to talk rather than listen.

---

43 Tannen, p.163.

- Restate some of what the person said – paraphrase. Often people are planning what they are going to say next rather than truly listening. If you decide you are going to paraphrase some of what you hear, you are forced to pay close attention. Your first reaction when you try paraphrasing may be that it is redundant and a waste of time, but you will be amazed at how much the speaker will appreciate it. Sometimes their eyes light up with surprise because so few people have ever demonstrated that they heard them.

I practice this most when I am doing career counseling.

Work example: After listening to a client for 15-20 minutes, I summarized this way: "Let me see if I have this straight – you are being excluded from meetings, the CEO said you are a dinosaur, you want to stay in Orlando, but you've checked with the competition and there are no openings. You have a possibility of a job in Seattle. I didn't hear an option in Orlando. Am I missing something?" He said, "No, I don't think so." That person needed to talk about his situation, hear himself say out loud the options rather than just having them rattle around in his head. He knew the next thing he needed to do. He just needed to talk to someone who was listening intently to help him clarify it.

Personal example: In this instance I didn't need to restate as much for her to feel I understood. I was listening while having dinner with a friend who was describing her stay at the Surf and Sand Motel in Laguna Beach. I responded to her detailed description, "You could almost touch the ocean out your balcony window. How wonderful."

In some circles giving feedback or paraphrasing is called active listening. "Active listening involves a restatement of either the message or the feeling of the speaker without giving advice, analyzing, or probing."[44] A particular phrase associated with active listening – I hear what you are saying – has been overused. Avoid it.

Active listening, paraphrasing, restating the gist of what they have said to you – whatever you want to call it – it is the place to begin when listening to someone with a problem. You do not want to interrupt quickly and say, "I know how you feel" or give advice. But you do not want to over do active listening either, because the listener may feel that you are acting like a parrot or a robot.

With loved ones, who already know I'm listening hard to them, I don't restate or paraphrase as much. I'm more likely to ask a question for clarification to draw out more of the story. I'll say, "That's great" or "I know that was tough". If you have not

---

[44] Carr, *Communicating and Relating*, p.52

been listening to family members and friends, paraphrasing is a helpful tool in gaining trust and convincing them that this time you truly are paying attention.

- Make a guess about a feeling. Mad, glad, sad, afraid covers most of the categories. If you say, "I can see why that would make you sad," you might get the response, "I'm not sad, I'm angry." It doesn't matter if you guess wrong. If you mention a feeling, they will tell you which one they are having and probably expound about the cause. This is a high form of listening and takes the most energy.

- Don't be thinking about when it is your turn to talk or what you are going to say when they stop. A client said to me, "When you talk, I'm actually reloading." Gallway in *The Inner Game of Work* said,

> *"People know when they are being given full attention. They also know when you are just waiting for them to finish so that you can make your point. When one person gives full attention to another, it tends to become contagious, affecting the quality of both participants' speaking and listening."*[45]

Particularly at work when people come to talk about a problem, we usually think – of course, they want me to solve it or why else would they be wasting my time? Often they want to work it out themselves, but they just wanted you to listen to them sound off about it. If I convince you to try this and when the person finishes talking, he/she asks you, "What do you think I should do?" and you don't know what to say, it is perfectly acceptable to say, "I'd like to think about what you said. Can I give you my reaction a little later?" Most people will be honored that you would take the time to think about your response.

Listening Takes Energy

Extraverts often have a harder time trying to listen than Introverts because they are more comfortable talking. However, it can also be tough for Introverts because they can be so good at retreating into their own inner world and tuning out everybody and everything around them. So almost everyone has some personal growth to do if they are going to be good listeners.

Don't think that you will listen well in all situations. What I am suggesting takes enormous energy, and you won't always want to expend it. However, I recommend when you can't listen, say so rather than pretend. Example: "I want to listen closely, but I can't right now. Can we set up a time when I can give you my undivided attention?"

---

[45] Gallwey, *The Inner Game of Work*, p. 69

However, listening behavior in meetings is a different story. We all do some pretending there. It is disruptive to everyone else who may still be listening to rear back in your chair, put your hands behind your head and let out a big sigh. The better part of valor there is to continue to pretend to listen. Others may still be tuned in and your display of boredom or fatigue is disruptive. Taking notes is a way to fight fatigue, to appear to or actually stay engaged when you are having trouble listening.

A cocktail party calls for less intense listening – particularly a networking cocktail party. The conversation is light, cursory. You listen as best you can with the background noise and don't expect heavy conversation. You are meant to move from person to person although I have never learned to do it without feeling like I have been rude and left the person behind in mid-sentence. But moving on is effectively working the room for business and/or social purposes.

Reasons to Stop Listening

There are two main reasons to stop listening – you are hurting yourself or you are not helping the speaker. Melody Beattie writes: "Many of us can quickly tell what someone else is feeling, why that person is feeling that way, how long they've felt that way, and what that person is probably going to do because of that feeling."[46] I can catch anxiety when I listen to someone because emotions are contagious. Overdoing listening can cause fatigue and eventually resentment. Know when enough is enough and do what you need to do to take care of yourself. I have to remind myself to listen for the feelings, be concerned, but not make them my own. I have to stay separate and set limits.

The second reason to stop listening is that more listening hurts the speaker. Speakers often talk because they need to make changes in their lives. They may have complained to you many times about a situation. Each time they do, they temporarily feel a little better, but the energy for making the change evaporates, and they do nothing. Sometimes not being able to tell it one more time causes the negative energy to build up enough steam that they do what they need to do to make a change – finish a project, quit a frustrating job, come up with a better parenting plan, go to counseling, or leave an emotionally or physically abusive relationship.

Saying you are not going to listen any more can seem abrupt and hurtful, so subtly back off a bit. Making yourself less available for conversations or responding less sympathetically can sometimes change the complaining communication pattern that has been established and cause the person to take needed action. Even if they do not change, it may

---

46 *Codependent No More, How to Stop Controlling Others and Start Caring for Yourself*, p.142.

be time for you to let the problem go for your own mental and physical health. When we "let go and let God," something good usually happens.

Getting Someone to Listen to You

I get listened to by my husband, daughter, son, daughter-in-law, mother, and a couple of friends. For an Introvert that is quite enough people.

At first, my husband was a better talker than listener, but he changed. His mother talked a lot, and he was used to tuning her out when he chose to. When we first got married, he did that with me at times, mostly out of habit, I think, because I am not a constant talker. He would look at the newspaper or his eyes would glaze over, and I knew he was mentally gone. After a few times, I realized what was going on, so whenever he did it, I stopped talking mid-sentence and left the room. He is a curious person. This was an unexpected action, so he would usually come find me to ask what I was saying.

A caveat here — I never ever try to have a conversation with him if he is watching a sports event. We regularly talk at dinner time so usually I can wait until then. Because I know we are going to talk and he will listen well then, I am not usually feeling a sense of desperation. If I am angry about something, I write it out in my journal and say, "When you are ready, I have something I need to talk to you about. I seldom have to wait. After many years of marriage, he knows something is up, and he usually wants to get the conversation over with."

Some of you may be thinking — if I walk away, he won't ever follow and ask me what I was saying. If that is true, the relationship you want is over or is not going to happen. My first marriage ended after two years. He never wanted to talk or listen. I cannot even nobly say I ended it. I did not have that kind of courage. I remembered my father's biting critical voice when he talked about divorced women, and in 1970, I thought divorce was unacceptable to my family.

When my first husband talked of separating, I cried constantly and said to a doctor, whom I had asked to give me some Valium, "I cannot be divorced," and he said, "Yes you can." When the marriage ended, I thought I could never have the husband and children I wanted, but I was wrong. I knew if I married again, at the top of the list of my requirements for a husband was someone who was willing to talk to me and listen. He has for over 30 years, and it is one of the greatest blessings of my life.

Listening is a Gift

When you decide to listen, you give the speaker a gift. I said at the beginning of this chapter that I learned to listen well out of a sense of fear. It started from fear, but it continues from enjoyment. As an Introvert, I find listening easier than having words to say in all situations. I regularly enjoy listening to family members, friends, and clients that I coach professionally.

In a house of worship you give the gift of listening with the hope of receiving comfort and courage in return. I listen better in church when the ministers risk telling something about their personal lives. If they never admit to struggling with life or faith, then I have nothing in common with them and just do not hear many of the words.

The ministers in my church have a history of intermittently sharing their struggles. One of them, Carlyle Marney, was there (1958-1967) before I moved to Charlotte the first time, but I heard him once on a recruiting trip and have read some of his books. He wrote in *The Recovery of the Person*, "Man, in the context of his antecedents, his society, history and biology (warts and all) is guilty, shamed and frightened. Always he is these, and almost nowhere dare he, can he tell about it."[47] We are all carrying stories about ourselves that need telling and healing. We need someone to hear them.

Marney also said, "This is the sovereign grace of God in persons that a man can be heard through anything, and once he has been heard, he is really never again as if he had not been heard."[48] I have been heard and healed because of it. In my first marriage I experienced not being heard and the deep injury that goes with it. When you can, give the gift of listening, and be grateful when you receive it.

---

[47] Marney, *The Recovery of the Person*, p.159.

[48] Marney, *The Recovery of the Person*, p.158.

Works Cited

Beattie, Melody. *Codependent No More, How to Stop Controlling Others and Start Caring for Yourself.* San Francisco: Harper San Francisco, 1992.

Carr, J. *Communicating and Relating.* Menlo Park, CA: Benjamin/Cummings Publishing, 1979.

Gallwey, W. Timothy. *The Inner Game of Work.* New York: Random House, 2000.

Marney, Carlyle. *The Recovery of the Person.* Nashville: Abingdon Press, 1963.

Kirschner, Dr. Rick and Dr. Rick Brinkman. *Life by Design: Making Wise Choices in a Mixed-Up World.* New York: McGraw-Hill, 1999.

Pitino, Rick with Bill Reynolds. *Success is a Choice.* New York: Broadway Books, 1997.

Swets, Paul. *The Art of Talking So That People Will Listen.* Englewood Cliffs, NJ: Prentice-Hall, 1983.

Tannen, Deborah, PhD. *That's Not What I Meant.* New York: Ballantine Books, 1986.

Chapter 5

Say What You Mean

Say what you mean, be as truthful as you can when it is appropriate, when it is worth the effort. There is no need to tell a person her hair looks awful or his clothes are a mess. I am not suggesting cruel honesty. In social groups some little white lies are necessary to be polite and civil. You can choose to say nothing rather than speak up and unnecessarily hurt someone's feelings. If you dislike an in-law, it is not a good idea to regularly tell a family member who doesn't share your sentiment. However, on the big issues, the concerns that really matter to you, you need to speak up.

Be as clear as you can when you decide to have an important conversation. Here's an example of when I began to do this:

When my children were five and two, I lay on the bed and cried for two hours. I felt I was raising them alone while my husband worked and then played golf. He was providing well for us as a pediatrician, and I was working under the notion that my half of the equation was that I did everything in the parenting area.

However, I was exhausted and bitter and taking my anger out on my daughter who I thought was extremely demanding. I went to counseling and realized the problem was not my daughter. I was the problem. I did not calmly set limits with her, her Dad, or myself. After the crying jag that Sunday afternoon, I began to find ways to say what I wanted and describe some consequences if I didn't get some help.

As I wallowed on the bed, I tried to think of one thing I wanted to do, and I could not. I could, however, think of one thing I did not want to do. I did not want to cook supper, and I decided I wouldn't. I knew this would begin a discussion.

As I said earlier I have been married for a long time. My first marriage of two years right after college ended in divorce. I was devastated and thought I could not have any of the things I wanted most in life at that time – a husband and children.

I thought this confrontation would be the beginning of the end of my second marriage. I did not want that, but I would not keep living like I was. So the risk for this confrontation felt extremely high. I was afraid but determined. I had been writing about this for days in my journal.

So I said nothing, but I didn't cook. My husband came to me, asking, "When are we having supper?"

I replied, "I'm not fixing it."

"Why not?"

I said, "I don't like how things are going around here, and I want to talk about changing them. You play golf many afternoons after work and both weekend days. I take care of two children and cook supper. I want to do things my way three nights a week, your way three nights, and we'll negotiate the other night. My way means you come home, take care of children while I fix supper. You put them to bed. If we don't do this, there will be no cooking." Amazingly, the evening meal was very important to him.

There were more words than these, but I had gotten clear on what I meant, said it, and began an enormous change in how we related to each other. Prior to that I had gone along, put up with stuff, and generally tried to please everyone around me. This may not seem like such a big deal, but it was huge to me. I thought such confrontations brought about the end of a marriage. They had before, and I thought they would again.

However, it was not the end. It was the beginning of equality and balance that needed to have been there all along, but I had been too scared to stand up for it due to fears left over from my first marriage and some unpleasant conversations with my father. Up until then, I had assumed I knew how my husband would respond, and I was wrong. He was willing to meet me half way.

As the years went by, I experienced the raising of children as being easier every year. Once they reached the age where we could have a conversation about slicing the sandwich the wrong way and then fixing another one if they were having a bad day, I did not feel the same level of desperation and need for help.

When my son started kindergarten, I felt an enormous freedom as I watched him walk down the sidewalk holding his sister's hand. I had six hours each day to spend however I chose. I had already started graduate school when he was two so I had plenty to do, but there was something magical about six uninterrupted hours to think.

I continued to negotiate when I needed more help from my husband, but since our children have been grown, I love that he plays golf because it gives me the solitude I need for writing and creativity. It is very healing for me to be in our house alone. So if you want change, it is important to say what you mean when you need to.

What to Say — Ways to Get Prepared

It is a good idea to prepare for important conversations. By freewriting ahead of time, you can clearly focus on what you want and what price you are willing to pay to get it. Think about a communication situation that you would like to change. Freewrite answers to the following questions:

- What do you think about the situation?
- What do you feel about the situation?
- What do you want?
- What will be the good or bad consequences if you get it?
- What are you willing to do to get what you want?
- What do you think the other person wants?
- Can you give him/her any of what he/she wants?
- What will you do if you do not get what you want?

Example:

I coached a physician executive who needed to have a conversation with a physician who was yelling at co-workers when things didn't go well in the operating room. Here are the answers to his preparation questions:

- **What do you think about the situation?** I think he gets scared when a case is not going well, and he screams to relieve his own fear.

- **What do you feel about the situation?** I'm aggravated that he can't behave like everyone else does. I'm annoyed that I have to confront him. I am a little afraid of what his reaction will be.

- **What do you want?** I want him to firmly ask for what he wants and needs in that situation without screaming.

- **What will be the good or bad consequences if you get it?** Good — I'd stop getting complaints. Everyone would function better in the operating room because they aren't afraid of how he will explode. Bad — he might not do as well in the case if he doesn't release the tension. He might get mad and take his business across town to the other hospital.

- **What are you willing to do to get what you want?** Have the conversation. I would say, "Jim, I heard you yelled at Mary in the operating room." I listen while he complains about many things. "This is the 2nd time this month." He complains. "Our recently revised code of conduct is quite clear about this being unacceptable behavior. I want to tell you about some consequences if this happens again."

- **What do you think the other person wants?** To be bossy to others. To do well in cases.

- **Can you give him/her any of what he/she wants?** I can work on the system problems he has complained about, but I cannot allow this behavior anymore. We are going to get sued.

- **What will you do if you do not get what you want?** If he doesn't change this behavior after three conversations about it, I will start the process to get his privileges suspended.

You will not use this kind of energy to get ready for every conversation, but if it is a significant one or a topic you've covered several times without good results, then think hard, get ready, write out what you want to say. Do some pre-thinking with the questions. Then decide if you are going to have the conversation. Sometimes you won't because after writing about the bad consequences, you'll decide the risk is too great. It is wonderful to have thought it through before you are in the middle of a conversation and say things you may regret.

If you decide you are going to have the conversation, then thoroughly prepare. Even write about how you think the other person might respond to what you say and then write how you hope to respond. You can't take your notes with you and you don't need to. Something about writing it down gets it clear and firmly implanted in your brain. It also helps reduce anxiety which enables you to better handle the conversation when it actually happens.

How to Say It

Use Good Body Language.

How you say something and how you look when you say it are as important as what you say. What causes someone to understand you and respond well to you? Psychologist Albert Mehrabian in a famous 1971 study, "...found that seven percent of understanding depends on the words you use, 38 percent depends on your tone of voice, and 55 percent depends on your nonverbal body language.[49]

Facial expression and voice communicate much more than you realize. A listener understands and interprets your message more through the tone of your voice and the look of your body than through your words. "No, I'm not angry!" said harshly conveys the message that you are angry. "I really love that!" said sarcastically implies that you don't like it at all. People complain about getting mixed signals when words, tone of voice, and body language send different messages. They will believe the voice, face, and body much more than the words you say.

Joe Alexander, in *Dare to Change*, claims people have a hard time accepting these facts. "The reality is that few people accept responsibility for anything more than their words. They have never learned that a harsh tone can deny the gentlest of words...."[50] Many people refuse to believe it if they are the ones doing the talking, but they quickly believe it if someone else is talking.

Your face should generally look cheerful or kind unless sternness and discipline are called for. Being in control of your body will help you control the message so you have a better chance of being understood. Don't fiddle with your hair, your beard, or a paper clip. Don't open mail, read email, glance at the newspaper, have the TV on in the background or have a conversation in a crowded hallway. Turn your body, energy, and attention toward the other person to get your message across clearly.

Strive for eye contact 80% of the time. Don't have a staring contest. It's natural to look away and think, but then look back at the person. Looking at the ceiling or over someone's shoulder makes them think you are not really interested in talking to them.

Paul Swets described positive and negative body language:

> "A positive voice is cheerful, satisfied, concerned, warm. A negative voice is sarcastic,
> scared, depressed, clipped, tense, too loud or soft. A positive face has a smile, an
> occasional head nod, and eye contact. A negative face has a frown, smirk, or boring

---

49 J. Griffin, *How to Say It at Work*, p.17.
50 Alexander, p.138.

glare. A positive body is relaxed, leaning forward some, with open arms. Negative body language is pointing, wandering eyes, picking at your body."[51]

Be even more careful about your tone of voice when you talk on the telephone. We are often thrown into people's voice mail unexpectedly if their line is busy. Do not leave a stumbling, mumbling message. If you are not prepared to be concise and sound intelligent, hang up the phone, write out what you want to say and call back to leave the message. Recruiters, customers, your boss, your co-workers, friends, even your family members will make judgments about your competency by the quality of your voice and the coherence of your message.

When you leave a voice mail, say your phone number slowly and more than once. Some people say their number so fast it seems they are trying to impress me with how smart they are. Don't do it. Make listeners grateful that they only have to listen to the message once to get the numbers written down.

Avoid Big Emotions.

Try to avoid big emotions – anger and tears. They usually interfere with communication. You can certainly feel and express big emotions if you are by yourself. Write them out or yell them when you are driving or at home alone. But calm down before you have the conversation. The listener is often threatened, frightened, or repulsed by a show of uncontrolled emotion. He or she cannot hear the words being spoken. The person raging usually overstates the case. The one crying understates it and can't get the words out.

If you have a tendency to blow up when stressed, figure out what usually happens right before you lose your cool. It might be a flushed face or a suddenly rigid body caused by the lightning-speed surge of adrenaline coursing through your body. Let that be your warning signal to leave the situation or say, "I need a while to think about this."

Jerry Wisinski, in *Resolving Conflicts on the Job*, suggests saying,

> *"'Phil, this isn't getting us anywhere. Why don't we give it a rest for a while and discuss it later when we've both calmed down a little, OK?' When this approach is used, it is important that the person who calls the 'time out' initiate the issue again within an appropriate amount of time."*[52]

I have worked with physicians for almost 20 years. A surgeon who wants to scream cannot get away during an operation. Learning and regularly practicing relaxation and deep breathing exercises has helped some stop their outbursts. Also writing in private about

51 Paul Swets, *The Art of Talking So That People Will Listen*, p.59.

52 Wisinski, p.19.

all the things that make them angry can diffuse some of the hot emotion when they are with people who aggravate them.

John Sanford describes this helpful process:

> "Writing in our journal about people or situations that have evoked in us anger, anxiety, or a sense of defeat helps to stabilize our psychological situation and strengthen our ego. It helps us to 'get a handle' on our emotions without repressing them, and to get a look at the giant that threatens to swallow us. If we do this before we get into a discussion that might become highly emotional, the chances are good that we can express our feelings to the other person and not be consumed by them."[53]

There are times when it is appropriate to cry as a needed emotional and physical release – in a grief situation, when someone's words touch you deeply, even when you are over-joyed, but if you cry regularly at work, people tend to not respect your opinions. If you feel the tears about to spill over, go to the bathroom, run cold water on your wrists, or go for a walk if you can.

Sometimes you can stop the tears with a very simple technique of saying and doing the following words: I am breathing in, I am breathing out, I am relaxing.[54]

I used to cry when I got angry. A friend said to me once, "I think anger is unacceptable to you, and you switch over to tears and lose your power." I was furious with him for saying it but gradually realized he was right. It was not acceptable in my growing up household to express anger, particularly to my father. Writing out what I am going to say in my journal, even writing both sides of the dialogue – I say, he says – prepares me to say what needs to be said without crying.

If you are with someone who is crying, try to wait it out, and then still talk. Anytime you can sit with someone who cries, hand them a tissue, and wait until they can go on, you have given that person a tremendous gift. When there is crying, it is often women who are doing it and men who are hating it. Some men seem so frightened or repulsed by tears, they almost seem to think the person is going to melt. Not true.

However, some people use tears to manipulate. Every time you try to have a difficult conversation, they cry to try to scare you off. You must have it anyway. If you work or live with someone who cries every time you bring up a difficult subject, you simply will have to get used to the tears and carry on with the conversation.

If you are on the receiving end of big emotions, there are two approaches you can take.

---

53 J. Sanford, *Between People: Communicating One-to-One*, p.37.

54 Maxie Maultsby in *Coping Better...Anytime, Anywhere* describes this slow breathing as step one in his Rational Behavior Therapy, p.35.

If you are the listener and are feeling strong and collected, it can be helpful if you can let the emotional person vent or cry for a few moments. If they are angry, you might then respond, "I can see that you are angry and I'm not surprised. What can I do to help?" If they are crying, you can be still.

If you are not up to being in the presence of so much negative energy, you might say one of the following:

"I'll be glad to talk about this when you are not yelling."

"I can meet with you this afternoon at 3:00 in my office."

"Your loud voice keeps me from hearing your words."

"Your tears — pick one — unnerve me, scare me, confuse me, cause me to cry." (Sometimes naming the emotion reduces its power.)

The big emotions of anger and tears can interfere with good communication. Decide which troubles you the most whether you are on the giving or the receiving end and come up with a plan to deal with it.

For example, I can easily sit with people when they cry, but I am very uncomfortable when loud disagreements are going on. My tendency is to leave the situation unless I am being paid to help resolve the conflict or it's a family member to whom I am committed. I don't even like being at the dining room table when guests are having a heated debate. I'll go to the bathroom, decide if it is important for me to hang in no matter how loud things get. If yes, then I brace myself for whatever comes. If no, I clear the dishes. However, if I am managing a conflict situation at work, I stay and keep saying calmly, firmly, and sometimes repeatedly, what needs to be said.

Be Very Careful About Teasing.

My first teasing came from my older brother and my father. I learned to ignore my brother, but not so much my father. When I was 14, I began to work in his grocery store each summer. At first I wrapped meat, but later I moved up to the cash register to enter in each grocery item and check customers out. This was in the days before cashiers scanned bar codes. Items would often be priced to encourage customers to buy more. I remember 6 cans of tomato sauce for 85 cents. If the person bought 2 cans, I would pause trying to figure out what each can would be. Once my Dad was watching, called out 15 cents for the first, 14 for each of the rest, and laughingly said, "All that fancy math you've taken, and you can't do simple arithmetic." Shame radiated through my body, and I wanted to disappear into the floor. Teasing hurts even more if it's true, and almost all teasing has a grain of truth in it — to this day math problems can make me break out in a sweat.

Not everyone agrees with me about the negative effects of teasing. My husband loves it. His day doesn't feel complete without a certain quota of horsing around with his friends. It seems essential nourishment for his psyche. However, he is careful about teasing me much because he knows how I feel about it.

If you and a coworker are both enjoying the teasing, it can still make the people around you uncomfortable. They worry it can happen to them, and they think you don't respect people.

Those, who are good at teasing, love it; those, who are not, hate it and plot revenge. Teasing can be fun between people of equal power and status, but often it is a secret form of aggression and strips its victim of power unless both parties are equally good at the quick barb. Teasing usually allows the one doing the teasing to feel one up. This feels good to the teaser, but it eliminates closeness and can build resentment.

If you are in a relationship you think is equal but you are doing all the teasing, it usually means the other person is not good at it. The two of you are not equal in the ability to participate in the banter.

If you tease your children a lot, you may want to rethink that. You are not equals. The child usually feels very bad even though he or she may be forced to laugh because the teaser will say, "Can't you take a joke?" If you tease subordinates, there also is a good chance you are enjoying it more than they are.

Gordon MacKenzie in *Orbiting the Giant Hairball* says "Teasing is a disguised form of shaming." A man in a group he was working with said, "Wait a minute. Teasing is how I show affection." MacKenzie's response was, "You must find a better way."[55]

I am not good at teasing, but I can laugh at myself. For example, I spent time and money decorating my guest bathroom perfectly so the women who came to my New Years Eve party would "ooh and ahh" when they came out of it. It had navy blue walls with white trim, a burgundy, navy, and white oriental rug, gold mirror, brass sconces, burgundy towels, cute soap dish and ceramic tissue box cover.

Thirty minutes before everyone arrived, the toilet backed up and began overflowing. The sink and tub were filling up. I grabbed a kitchen pan. My husband used it to dip out the toilet. My daughter yanked the rug out of the bathroom. My future daughter-in-law went

---

55 MacKenzie, *Orbiting the Giant Hairball*, pp.121-123.

to the store to get Draino. My son turned the water off leading to the toilet and sink. Everyone yelled and scrambled. We had to put a sign on the door that directed people to the upstairs bathroom which was not decorated. In the middle of it all, I heartedly laughed and said to all my family members helping me clean up the mess, "This is an existential moment. You can fix your bathroom perfectly, but you can't necessarily show it off. The s*** will back up." It would have been entirely different if one of the family members teased me during the clean up, but nobody did.

In general, I think people have fear simmering just below their consciousness that others will humiliate them for the way they look, what they say, or what they have done. They cope with this in several ways. Some try to do most of the talking which often includes teasing, some stay quiet, and others try to get away.

Eliminating teasing can restore balance in a relationship you are trying to improve. It can get you more of what you want — better behavior in children, better behavior in adults at work and at home.

Anger, tears, and teasing are the big emotional issues to consider when talking. Now let's think about techniques that make you an effective speaker.

Use a Moderate Speaking Pace.

People speak at different speeds depending on their location in the country, their culture, age, even their gender. We all have our own natural speaking speed, but sometimes we need to be flexible and adjust to fit a particular situation.

Kurt Lewin, a social scientist, devised a formula B=f(PE), to represent his idea that (B) behavior is a function of (P) personality interacting with (E) the environment.[56] Think of going to a football game and a house of worship. You may have prayed at a football game, but you probably haven't jumped up and yelled "kill 'em" in a house of worship. You are the same person, but because you are in a different environment, you behave differently.

So change your pace to fit the environment or the person. Speak slower in a house of worship. If you are adding to or taking away from someone's belief system, they need time to absorb the emotional impact. Pick up the pace in the northeast region of the United States, or they will think you are slow and dimwitted. If five people who speak before you on a panel have a much faster pace than you, try to pick yours up as much as you can or the audience may tune you out before they hear any content. I have spoken regularly to physician executives who demand a fast pace.

---

56 Kurt Lewin, *Principles of Topological Psychology*, p. 12.

Manny Elkind says, "It is easy to imagine that you would talk differently to your grandmother than you would to a three-year old. When you are flexible in your speaking style, you are not phony, you are being strategically appropriate."[57]

Speak Loudly Enough.

Your voice should be loud enough to be easily heard but not shrill or attacking. Use your lips and tongue. I took a voice and articulation class in which we did warm up exercises for our voices — body and mouth stretches, humming sounds, and quick repetitions of phrases such as — bumpy baby buggy. Articulate with enough volume if you want people to pay attention to you.

When people speak too softly, they drain energy from the listeners by causing them to have to strain to hear the words.

However, don't do the reverse and talk too loudly. If people think you are yelling at them, they will try to get away from you or become equally loud. Not much good happens once the screaming begins.

Don't let the pitch rise at the end of the sentence. When the voice goes up at the end of a statement, the words, no matter what the meaning, sound like a question asked without confidence. I've heard this habit most often from teenage girls when they are copying "Valley Girl" talk. It sends the message of insecurity no matter what the age or gender. When teenage boys are not speaking well, their problem seems to be mumbling. We all go through some stages developmentally that we need to give up in the grown-up workplace.

During presentations, seminars, lectures, or sermons, people feel led and supported by a confident strong voice. It momentarily allays their fears. The subconscious sensation they feel is: This person knows what she/he is talking about and can take care of me for the next few minutes.

One of my favorite ministers, Gene Owens, had a deep melodious voice with no accent but with the good pace of the South — slow enough to absorb the meaning, but not so slow that the congregation rushed ahead when we all said the Lord's Prayer together. I felt he was in control, not letting me fall. He was able to tell a story deliberately without leaving out an essential detail but not tell so much that I was overburdened. The sound of his voice was rich and deep as if from a long vertical well that says — I have felt pain and survived. At appropriate times he could laugh and have a bright twinkle in his eye that let me know I was going to enjoy what was coming.

---

[57] Manny Elkind, *Certified Physician Executive Tutorial Presentation*, March, 2002

Be Concise and Specific.

Use fewer words rather than more. If you talk too long and give people too much information, they will tune you out. At work, colleagues consider it wasting time and keeping them from getting their jobs done. At play, people consider it selfish or boring. My son, a minister, said if you make a sermon too long you snuff out the fire you have built.

It's especially important to be concise when giving feedback. Perhaps you need to talk to co-workers about behavior you want them to change. A natural tendency is to put the conversation off, store up resentment until you have a long list of mistakes and then in great exasperation go in and dump everything on them. At this point, they may have done 18 things you don't like, but you cannot tell all of them. Pick one or two.

When giving feedback, be concise in that you don't talk about too many issues, but also be specific. You may need to use more words to specifically describe what you don't like or what you like. In the following examples the first bullet is general and vague, the second bullet uses specific words to describe behavior.

Feedback — How <u>Not</u> to Do It and Then How to Do It:

Negative Feedback

- Don't say, "Your co-workers are mad at you because you don't treat them with respect."

- Describe what they don't like. "When Jim came to talk to you about the budget, he said you interrupted him after two sentences and said, 'You are crazy if you think I'm going to give you that much money.'"

Positive Feedback:

- Don't just say, "You did a good job."

- Describe what you like. "You didn't want to take the job as nurse manager, and, yet, you are doing a great job of scheduling, listening to the complaints, and being the back-up, on-call nurse."

Positve Feedback:

- Don't just say. "Alan, I appreciate what a generous person you are..."

- Describe what you like: "Alan, I appreciate the way you took all that time to fill me in on what I missed. It made a real difference to me."[58]

---

[58] Kegan and Lahey, *How the Way We Talk Can Change the Way We Work*, p. 100.

If you are specific, people can understand and absorb the compliment more and will give you more of the positive behavior you have described.

Pay attention to how you give feedback. Excessive meanness is not rewarded by the universe. Neither is placating niceness. Strive for a mid-range, calm, confident request without underlying venom. For example: "When you present your good ideas in meetings, I think you will be listened to better if you use fewer words. State your point and wait. Don't repeat your idea in different words."

However, there is a limit to how often you should give feedback. If you ask someone to change behavior and they don't do it, you want to eventually stop asking. If you have no negative consequences that you can evoke, face up to the fact that you cannot fix the situation. I'll say what I want two times, occasionally three. Your maximum may be higher, but set a limit. If you keep asking for a change and you can do nothing about it if the person doesn't, then you come across as begging, whining, or nagging. It is better to ignore the situation than keep calling attention to your lack of power. And sometimes letting it go will change the situation in unexpected positive ways.

Different Styles of Extraverts and Introverts

Extraverts talk quickly and say what they mean at the time, though they may change their minds after a lengthy conversation. Introverts have plenty of opinions formulated in quiet times, but they may take too long to voice them. Extraverts often shoot from the hip and have messes to clean up. It is as hard for them to not say exactly what is on their minds as it is for Introverts to speak up immediately.

Sometimes Extraverts will need to slow down a bit and not say everything they think as soon as it occurs to them. Sometimes Introverts will need to speed up a bit and tell what they are thinking before they have time to think it through entirely to see if it is safe to venture forward.

As an Introvert saying what I mean is the hardest instruction I give myself. I think of what I should have said an hour, a day, or a week later. I think of it but don't want to risk saying it. Writing in my journal what I want to say or don't want to say can help me get back in the conversation and get the words out to say what I mean.

Works Cited

Alexander, Joe. *Dare to Change*. New York: New American Library, 1984.

Elbow, Peter. *Writing Without Teachers*. New York: Oxford University Press, 1973.

Elkind, Mansfield, *Certified Physician Executive Presentation*, Hilton Head, SC, March 2002.

Kauer, Robert, "Business Plans and Projects," Sr. Lecturer, Dept of Banking and Finance, Weatherhead School, Case Western Reserve University, Cleveland, OH. *Certified Physician Executive Tutorial*, Feb., 2002, Tampa, FL.

Kegan, Robert and Lisa Laskow Lahey. *How the Way We Talk Can Change the Way We Work*. San Francisco, CA: Jossey-Bass, 2001.

Griffin, J. *How to Say It at Work*. Paramus, NJ: Prentice Hall Press, 1998.

Lewin, Kurt. *Principles of Topological Psychology*. New York: McGraw-Hill, 1936.

MacKenzie, Gordon. *Orbiting the Giant Hairball, A Corporate Fool's Guide to Surviving with Grace*. New York: Viking, 1998.

Maultsby, Maxie C., Jr., MD. *Coping Better...Anytime, Anywhere, The Handbook of Rational Self-Counseling*. Bloomington, Indiana: Rational Self-Help Books, 1986.

Sanford, J. *Between People: Communicating One-to-One*. New York: Paulist Press, 1982.

Stettmer, M. *The Art of Winning Conversation*. Englewood Cliffs, NJ: Prentice Hall, 1995.

Swets, Paul. *The Art of Talking So That People Will Listen*. Englewood Cliffs, NJ: Prentice-Hall, 1983.

Wisinski, Jerry. *Resolving Conflicts on the Job*. New York: Amacom, 1993.

Chapter 6

Work When You Need To

I love having a job and making money. I also love time off to write, putter around, do crafts, and see family. Life balance, which almost everyone says they want, requires working enough to do the job well and feel satisfied with your accomplishments, but also learning when not to work.

Think about your work history. Here's mine. I taught high school English for four years after I graduated from college. Then I had children which was more work than I had ever known, but it was inside the home and unpaid. When they were five and two, I started graduate school, got an MA in English and began adjunct teaching of Freshman English in four different colleges. I wanted to be a full-time professor, so for three years I took courses in an English PhD program to try to make it happen. At the same time I taught Business Writing for the American Management Association in seminars all over the country. Then a man I had known for 15 years offered me a full-time job to teach communication skills to physicians who were moving into administrative positions, which brings me to today.

I have felt blessed to have that job every day since I got it in 1990. It has allowed me to work from a home office, go to the main office when needed, and travel. I love most parts of my job:

- Seminar teaching where I give good, time-tested information about communication skills and tell parts of my own story about how I have communicated well and when I haven't.

- Career counseling with physicians who are deciding they want to do something besides be a practicing clinician when people around them are saying they are crazy not to be satisfied with what they have.

- Writing when it is going well or "having written" when it is not going well, but managing to get something on paper because I kept trying.

There are parts of my job I am not fond of: email because it multiplies like rabbits no matter what I do and some meetings.

Every job has some combination of likes and dislikes. That's a concept that mature people come to accept. My mother told me, "Whatever job you have, give it your best no matter how you feel about it because it will lead to the next good thing in ways you cannot foresee." That advice has spurred me on and proved true many times. I have added my own thought to her good one — give it the best you have each day. None of us are at our best every day, but if you are trying with a good attitude, it will usually be enough to keep you in the game even if you have some off days.

Think back over your work history. Do you see a natural progression that is satisfying to you or do you see repeated behaviors you would like to stop?

Working Too Much

Some people work all the time and don't know when to stop, and others don't work enough to get the job done. It is essential to find the right balance to do well in your job, stay healthy, and care for your important relationships.

Working all the time can feel good, chase away scary thoughts, make money, and get you out of unpleasant family confrontations. Bosses, or family members if you work inside the home, usually love your results. In fact, some organizations will cheerfully work you into the grave if you let them. Co-workers, children, spouses, relatives will let you sacrifice and wait on them until you drop. Only you can say when enough is enough, and it is vitally important that you learn to do it, say it to yourself and out loud, and have the courage to enforce it. Seldom will anyone say, "Here, sit down, take it easy, you have done more than your share." You have to say it yourself and live with the disapproval you may get.

If you are a people-pleaser like I am, you may have set up many situations at home and at work where you are doing too much for others.

As a Feeling type I love harmony. When the family comes for Christmas holidays, I want them all to be happy, and I used to try to make it happen. I was like a little radar machine sending out invisible tentacles to each person to see how they were doing and monitor their pleasure pulse. If they weren't happy, I'd try to do something about it. As you might guess, after five to seven days of this, I'd get tired, resentful and sometimes mean. Any good behavior taken too far can be harmful to yourself and others.

Although it is always my tendency to be a pleaser, I've learned to do this behavior less. One counselor gave me this instruction: the whole holiday in every situation, ask yourself — What would make me happy? Then do it. This was a radical shift for me, but, oddly enough, it led to more harmonious visits.

At work I said yes to every request. I should have stopped teaching seven-hour-a-day seminars long before I did. I had plenty of energy for the first 3 ½ to 4 hours, but then after the lunch break, it took grit and determination to keep my energy at the same level. The tension eventually took its toll, and I got sick. I was so busy traveling and teaching, I didn't take time to figure out that the stress was hurting my body.

Working Too little

While working too much can be harmful to your health, working too little won't get you the results you want in life. You must be willing to work enough to get the job done well, to get the education you need. When my daughter was in the 7th grade, in a fit of rebellion, she suddenly stopped studying. I said to her, "You have a great brain in your head. There is the history book on your desk. Good grades cannot happen if you don't open that book and put the information in that brain. Good grades are necessary to get what I think you want in the long run." Studying in the early years and working in the later years are necessary to get what most of us want out of life.

If you can get a task done in six hours when it would take someone else ten hours, count yourself among the very lucky. However, if it takes you ten and a friend six, don't whine about the unfairness of life. Work the ten it takes and be grateful. We are all given different talents, strengths and weaknesses. The only failure is not to use what you were given to the fullest.

Everyone I've talked to lately feels more insecurity and frustration about his or her job than they did a few years ago. And yet my mother reminds me it is hard to feel more insecurity than her generation did when they were starting out under the pall of the Depression.

In all times work is hard. That is why they call it work. People are aggravating. Some deadlines are impossible to meet. Children are unrelenting in their demands. It's the boss's job to suck every ounce of creativity and productivity out of you that he or she can get. If you don't have a boss, then the financial "wolf at the door" stands ready to knock all the time and take your business under. Some tolerate the freedom and risk of running their own businesses well. Others do not.

So work can be hard and stressful, but it can also be exhilarating and rewarding if you are doing what you feel called to do.

The Terkels in *Small Change* wrote, "Look for the connection between your work and the lessening of someone's suffering."[59] I work in the health care field providing management education to physicians who have leadership positions in their organizations. Here is a fantasy I use when I need to remind myself that the work I'm doing might be reducing someone's suffering:

If a physician leader confronts another physician who yells at a nurse, and he/she can convince that physician to stop behaving abusively, the work life of the nurse improves. The nurse feels better and may care for a patient with more accuracy and compassion. Even the stress level of the doctor may be reduced. Most doctors know yelling is inappropriate, and they bounce between anger and guilt when they do it. It is not a comfortable ride.

The "kick-the-dog" syndrome exists in families and at work. I know the truth of this old saying because I mistreated a dog when I wasn't handling the stress of little children well. If you can stop it at the top, the better behavior may filter down. The possibility of helping stop abusive behavior anywhere reminds me that my work is worth the effort.

While aspects of work are hard, that doesn't mean you should do too little of it. And too much, can cause imbalance that can harm your health or relationships. So let's think about reasons that we do work.

Why Work?

Many of us never stop to ask the question, "Why do we work?" or if we do, the quick assumption is, "Well, I have to or I can't live or someone has to take care of these children." Money is at the top of the list but there are also other reasons:

Work To Make Money.

Our first order of business is to pay the rent or mortgage, buy food, and clothe our bodies. If we are fortunate enough to do that, plus have some discretionary money, we need to decide what to do with it. Jerry Gillies in *Money-Love* talks of ways to feel positively about both saving money and spending it for pleasure. He recommends when you save

---

[59] Terkel, Susan and Larry. *Small Change*, p.224.

money that you visualize saving it for pleasure, not for illness or emergencies. Keep three things in mind when you spend money. "If you spend money on an object that gives you no pleasure, and performs no useful service, and stimulates no new ideas, then you can consider your money exchanged for a poor bargain."[60] If spending money does one of those three things (gives you pleasure, performs a useful service or stimulates new ideas), then it is money well spent, and you should give up feelings of guilt. (I am not talking about pleasure to the point of addiction – drugs or excessive drinking. Even shopping, sports, or eating can be overdone and become harmful to yourself and others.)

Work to Have Something to Do

Without either paid work outside the home, unpaid work in the home, or volunteer work, how would we fill our days? I've talked to people who retired early to play all the golf they wanted. In one to two months they had accomplished it. They just couldn't play anymore day after day. They needed something else to do so golf could once again be a fun diversion.

Stories abound of the excessively rich who don't know what to do with themselves because they don't have to make a living.

Work is a privilege of the healthy – young, old or in between. If you've been sick or in an accident that required a lengthy recovery, you probably were grateful to get back to work. I cannot stand to watch day time TV because it reminds me of being in the hospital when flicking through the channels was the only thing I could do to distract myself from the pain after surgery.

That doesn't mean that you don't feel a bit of dread on Monday morning or the first day back after vacation. Most people will claim play is more fun than work, but playing all the time means the recreational activities can become unfulfilling and stale – not the needed variety in your life. I've heard a fortunate few claim their work is always play for them – some country music artists, investment bankers, high rolling entrepreneurs – but that is not true for most of us everyday. A helpful attitude is to be grateful for work without expecting it to always be thrilling.

Work to Combat Loneliness

We work so we can have a reason to be with people without needing a one-on-one intimate conversation every time we are together. Some co-workers may become friends. Even if they don't, the money we make allows us to do fun things with friends we have made outside of work.

---

[60] Gillies, Jerry. *Money-Love*, p.121.

We also need other people to get the job done. We must connect with them, get their ideas, benefit from their creativity and offer ours to them. I work alone out of my home office, but the calls and meetings on the phone with co-workers in the main office and clients all over the country connect me to the outside world in an essential way.

Work to Give to Others

If we have family, we like providing for their security if that is one of the reasons we work, but it's not the only one. Assuming survival needs have been met, if <u>all</u> money goes to family, the provider becomes resentful. But if some money is kept for personal pleasure, people generally enjoy the ability to take care of their loved ones. Even now that my children are grown, I enjoy being able to give them gifts when I choose to.

Timothy Gallwey in *The Inner Game of Work* says, "You can view...work as an expression of gratitude...as a meaningful contribution to others while bringing enjoyment, learning, and financial compensation."[61]

Those of us who can work need to give some of what we make to others who are not fortunate enough to get to work. The biblical advice of giving away a tenth is a good idea. If a tenth seems like too much, then find some way to give what you can — either money or time.

Work to Make a Difference and Be Remembered

Most of us want to feel we have made the world a better place by being here. It feels good to help improve the lives of others, and it gives us a bit of immortality to think we might be remembered after we are gone. Gillies wrote, "When Dr. Abraham Maslow studied self-actualized people, that tiny portion of the population who made the most of their human potential, he found that they all had some work they felt was worthwhile and important."[62]

Here are some things that I value and think could make a difference: raising my children as best I could, making contributions to the improvement of health care; helping people find career satisfaction; showing people a writing process that can be life enriching and healing.

Make your own list. It's important for you to be clear with yourself about what you value and how you want to make a difference. A quick way to check your values is to ask, "Where do I spend my time and money?" If you know that and write it down, you are less likely to make decisions that violate your values.

---

[61] Gallwey, *The Inner Game of Work* p. 84

[62] Gillies, Jerry, *Money-Love*, p.59.

Moving Up — Why work in management?

Having thought about some good reasons to work in any capacity, now let's think about promotions, moving up, getting to the top. Moving up in an organization usually means moving into management activities. It's important to think about whether you are suited for it.

Gillies, when discussing how to make more money, suggests an unusual question to spark creative answers. Instead of asking "How can I earn more money? ask "How can I have more fun?"[63] If you are heading toward management, you need to view some of the tasks as fun or you probably won't stay with it very long. Do you like the challenge of making meetings a bit shorter and more effective? Do you enjoy getting out in the organization and visiting with people — managing by walking around? Do you view being nice to people to get what you want as totally kissing up or do you think it is generally appropriate behavior that greases the wheels of civilized society? Do you get satisfaction and pleasure from speaking to groups — from showing off your confident voice with good information to inspire them?

Edgar Shein in a publication by Drake Bean Morin, an outplacement firm, describes the traits that are necessary for someone to enjoy and thrive in management — general management requires certain types of emotional competence:

> *"The capacity to be stimulated by emotional and interpersonal issues and crises rather than be exhausted or debilitated by them; the capacity to bear high levels of responsibility without becoming paralyzed; and the ability to exercise power and make difficult decisions without guilt or shame."[64]*

Just as you can't tell what marriage is like until you are married, you can't know how you will respond to management activities until you have done some of them. Schein described the tough part of management:

> *"Until a person actually feels the responsibility of committing large sums of money, of hiring and firing people, of saying 'no' to a valued subordinate, that person cannot tell whether he or she will be able to do it or will like doing it."[65]*

I've done enough management tasks to know I don't want it to be my full time job. Teaching and career counseling are more energizing to me.

Schein says you also need to decide how much the unpleasant parts of management tasks get you down.

---

63 Gillies, *Money-Love*, p.122.

64 Schein, *Career Anchors*, p.24.

65 Schein, *Career Anchors*, p.18.

> *"...one of the most difficult aspects of the job is functioning day after day without giving up, getting an ulcer, or having a nervous breakdown. The essence of the general manager's job is to absorb the emotional strains of uncertainty, interpersonal conflict, and responsibility."*[66]

There are plenty of bright, highly, motivated people who don't want to move up into top management. Teachers who want to continue to teach and not become a principal. Sales people who want to continue to sell and not be the district boss trying to motivate others to sell more. They like the contact with customers and enjoy closing the deal. The bigger salary is a strong siren, but if you'll miss what makes you happiest, it won't be worth it for long. I knew a physician who moved into administration, but then decided to scale back his management duties because he enjoyed teaching and patient care more.

As organizations have become flatter, there are fewer middle management positions but someone is still in the top slot. It is important to have people in those roles who enjoy the work and do it well. Do you want to be that person? If the answer is yes, go for it and accept with grace the good and bad tasks that come with it. If the answer is no, enjoy what you are doing and ignore the pressure when others imply you should want to move up. Practice a response and repeat as much as necessary. In my early teaching days when asked if I was interested in moving into administration, I said, "I love the <u>students</u> too much to leave teaching them behind." You fill in the blank for yourself and say it to anyone who hassles you.

Discover What You Are Meant to Do as Your Life's Calling.

Many professionals willingly spend 60 or more hours a week at work. Some people work 2 jobs trying to pay the bills. If work is a place where you just bide your time and wait for weekends and vacations, where you just make money to do and buy the things you need and want, you will feel cheated at the end and perhaps quite resentful while you are getting there.

I know there are those who have to stay in unpleasant jobs to survive, but I also know ones who have choices but stay out of habit or fear of change.

Think about these questions. What do you feel called to do? What will make you say at life's end, "I spent the time well; if you are a religious person, I did what God called me to do." David Whyte in *The Heart Aroused, Poetry and the Preservation of the Soul in Corporate America* said, "Preservation of the soul means the palpable presence of some sacred otherness in our labors, whatever language we may use for that otherness: God, the universe, destiny, life or love."[67]

---

66 Schein, p.24.

67 Whyte, *The Heart Aroused*, p.15.

If your soul is engaged, at the end of the day, week, or month, you probably will be able to say, "I have done more meaningful activities than non-meaningful, wasting-of-time busywork." The first year I was out of college I taught English to 11th and 12th grade high school students. For the first six weeks I went home everyday with a raging headache, took a two-hour nap and then spent the rest of the night preparing for the next day. As the year progressed I didn't have to work that hard every night, and I could ease up a little on being such a strict disciplinarian. I realized if I had one good day a month where I felt I had made a difference in a child's life, it was worth it to me to keep teaching.

What is your minimum quota for satisfaction? You have to decide how much and how often you have to find meaning to keep going. Now if I write three pages each morning before 8:30, no matter how the day goes I feel I have done something I wanted to do and am called to do. If I talk to someone on the phone or in a seminar and can help them come up with a plan for what they might try next to make their life/work more satisfying, I think I am contributing value to the universe. Gillies said, "There is no way you will ever be able to buy back enough pleasure to make up for what you missed by not enjoying your work."[68] While it may not be possible to enjoy work every day, you need to enjoy it some days or consider making a change if at all possible.

Slow the Pace and Search for Meaning

Slow down, search for meaning, think about what you like and don't like about your job, what's working and not working in your personal life. Barbara Sher in *I Could Do Anything If I Only Knew What It Was* wrote:

> "*Personal meaning connects your deepest gifts with the rest of the world. Whether you turn out to be a gardener or a builder, a film maker or a doctor – when you're doing the right work you will feel connected, both to your soul and to the world outside you.*"[69]

Finding meaning requires some quiet time for reflection. You can keep moving so fast with work, exercise, caring for children, cleaning house that there is no time to think. If you have all those obligations, trade off with a spouse or friend at least once a month and get a day alone. Go to a park or have everyone else go to the park and you spend time alone – if you can stay home without doing chores.

This will not feel good the first time you do it. David Whyte described why we resist slowing down to think about our jobs:

---

68 Gillies, *Money Love*, p.64.

69 Sher, *I Could Do Anything If I Only Knew What It Was* p.31.

"As the current catch phrase goes, we want to work smarter rather than harder. Yet all of us are familiar with frantic busyness as a state that continually precludes us from opening to the quiet and contemplation it takes to be smart. The fast-moving mind rebels against slowing the pace because it intuits that it will not only have to reassess its identity but also take time to recover and recreate, and of course when we are in the buzzing-worker-bee mode, that would be a loss of momentum difficult to justify. We do not even have time to find out if our momentum is taking us over the nearest cliff."[70]

Here is an example of my slowing down and finding meaning when I wrote in my journal in November 2004:

"I feel right when I am doing career counseling, writing, teaching, writing. How do I find meaning — by continuing to look for it and it usually means looking backward to evaluate what has happened. Why did I schedule ten days in a row of teaching in Ohio, Dallas, and Colorado? Because I wanted to get the hell out of Dodge, get away from seeing Mama every week, get away when my son was living at home for a summer internship. He wanted to be with his wife and child — not us. Get away from wanting things for my daughter. Maybe God was taking control of my brain and making something happen that would cause me to slow down. I was getting sick and tired of everything so I got sick. I might even have used the words "sick and tired." Books say this phenomenon is true, but it is flat amazing when I can look back and see what I was doing. And the guilt is awful — after all Mama had done for me for a lifetime, how could I have such thoughts. Love your neighbor, especially your family, as yourself. If you don't love yourself enough to take care of yourself, you have nothing to give anyone. So I can discover what to do to take care of myself, but I can't also have their approval for doing it."

In this rambling journal entry, I discovered some truths and then began to make adjustments in my life. I started going to see my mother every other week. The change restored me and helped me not to worry about her every day. One night we were talking about the premature death of a high school classmate of mine and how important it is to take care of yourself. I said, "On that note, I need to come every other week and call the other week." She said, "Take care of yourself first." Just as I have throughout my life, I got her support.

---

[70] Whyte, *The Heart Aroused*, p.99.

Your organization and your family may not want you to slow down and think because they may not like the ideas you come up with. Timothy Gallwey in the *Inner Game of Work* said co-workers and particularly bosses can "...assume that if you do not feel 'stressed out,' or 'burdened,' you aren't working hard enough or are probably not 'pulling your weight.'"[71] If this is true in your organization, you may have to occasionally participate in the talk of busyness that is the demanded norm, but do it quickly, get out of there, get back to real work, and shake off the conversation and feeling of franticness that you just participated in.

At one hospital where I consulted, long hours are expected. The management team tries to beat the CEO to work by 6:45am, stay until 6:00pm or later and come in on Saturday till about 1:00. Another organization has flex hours. The employees can start at 7:30 and work until 4:00 or 9:30-6:00 with the understanding that when there is more work to be done, they will stay until it gets done. The different start times spread out over the organization are 7:00, 7:30, 8:00, 8:30, 9:00, and 9:30. However this organization also has travel involved and when on the road the workday begins at 4:30am and sometimes ends at 9:00pm or later.

Getting the work done in any organization may require some early mornings, late nights, and weekends, but don't let that turn into the way it always is. Set a time limit. Don't buy into corporate chatter that brags about being at the office until 9:00pm. They might have been playing solitaire on the computer or worse for an hour of that time. Or even if they were truly working, their bodies will not tolerate that kind of abuse indefinitely. And as they get tired, they are not as productive or accurate.

After the completion of the next big project, take time off, pay attention to your family, paint something, read a book, go for a walk, watch TV, or just do nothing. I've read that we need work and love to be happy. If you are fortunate to have both in your life, you must make time for both.

You need to decide what you can tolerate from a physical and emotional standpoint, too. Then learn to say, "No," or "Enough is enough." Robert Louis Stevenson said, "To know what you prefer instead of humbly saying Amen to what the world tells you you ought to prefer, is to have kept your soul alive."[72]

---

71 Gallwey, p.98.

72 Robert Louis Stevenson quoted in Cameron's *The Artist's Way*, p.43.

Saying No Is Risky.

You have a right and an obligation to take care of yourself. Anne Lamonte describes how important it is to take care of your emotional space. Everyone should have limits on what other people can say or do to them:

> "...every single one of us at birth is given an emotional acre all our own. You get one, your awful Uncle Phil gets one, I get one, Tricia Nixon gets one, everyone gets one. And as long as you don't hurt anyone, you really get to do with your acre as you please. You can plant fruit trees or flowers or alphabetized rows of vegetables, or nothing at all. If you want your acre to look like a giant garage sale, or an auto-wrecking yard, that's what you get to do with it. There's a fence around your acre, though, with a gate, and if people keep coming onto your land and sliming it or trying to get you to do what they think is right, you get to ask them to leave. And they have to go because this is your acre."[73]

Figuring out how to take risks and yet protecting yourself at the same time is tricky business. You may be thinking – if you protect your emotional acre, it will get stomped on. A boss may fire you, yell at you, or make fun of you in front of others. You can take only so much abuse at work. If you've been asked by your boss to do something that you are unwilling to do or you think you are being regularly discounted, then you have a choice to make: You can do what's asked of you and not say what you think and want, or you can learn to ignore the behavior and find enough pleasure outside of work, or you can look for employment elsewhere.

If there are work tasks that you really want to do or don't want to do, if you don't pay attention, your body will eventually start to take care of the issue for you. You will get some version of sick – a physical problem will begin or return, you may get depressed, or participate in such compulsive work or play behaviors that you lose your family and friends.

You need to figure out what you want and don't want to do. I'm not talking about lazy, good-for-nothing, shiftless, never-want-to-work, do-what-you-always-want behavior. (You can tell I've heard quite a few descriptors in my life.) Sometimes we have to suffer for a while to get something we truly want – get the education required to be a teacher, doctor, minister, manager, computer programmer, nurse; care for a newborn who requires constant attention and allows no uninterrupted sleep for months before you get the feedback of a coveted smile.

---

[73] Lamont, Anne. *bird by bird, Some Instructions on Writing and Life*, p.44.

But, if when you have the job you wanted, you find you dread everything about it, some changes have to be made no matter how much time and money you spent getting there or who thinks you should finally shut up and be happy because of all the sacrifices they have made on your behalf. I have counseled physicians who were shocked that they didn't like practicing medicine. Their families were not happy to hear it.

Try making some minor changes before you consider the major move of changing jobs: take a day off from work every week and don't read email, listen to voice mail, or turn on your cell phone — tell only one person where you are in case of an emergency. One Saturday a month let your spouse take the children away for a day or you go away for a day or get a baby sitter.

You may be able to compensate for work you don't like but need to continue for the paycheck by engaging in a passionate pursuit outside of work — quilting, training for a marathon, being a big brother or sister to a needy child, going to flea markets on the weekends, watching TV — Nascar races, football, basketball, baseball, golf, the home decorating channel, Animal Planet, the soaps you recorded while you were at work.

Sometimes you can move decisively when you realize how unhappy you are, but if the risk of losing your job is high, you may need to keep your plans secret for a while. No job is perfect but you need to consider how much dissatisfaction you can stand.

What you are willing to risk may depend on how many financial obligations you have: How big is your mortgage? Do you have to educate children or make car payments? What would it cost to buy your own health insurance?

One woman hated her job but decided to keep it so her daughter could go to college. In four years she would reassess her situation.

The big issue may be that you would be embarrassed to be out of work and fear having a gap in employment on your resume. It may be a question of power — I like having my own money to spend as I please. I show a great deal of restraint in spending it, but I make that decision — no one else.

Some people have to be fired before they dare ask themselves the questions — What do I want? Where is my soul leading me? What am I called to do? I recently talked to a man who said his wife does not want him asking such questions, and he wouldn't be doing it if he hadn't just lost his job. Even while we keep a job, we need to occasionally imagine how we could thrive without it and ask ourselves — what else could we do?

David Whyte said, "To live with courage in any work or in any organization, we must know intimately the part of us that does not give a damn about the organization or the work."[74]

If You Decide You Need to Change Jobs

Suppose you decide there is no way you can find satisfaction or emotional and physical health in your present job. As you plan career moves, do some writing to explore your motives. Laura Day in *Practical Intuition for Success* said, "...history's most creative and productive individuals, from daVinci to Edison, all kept journals to record their observations, and even minor thoughts. Journals are undeniably an excellent way for you to gain access to your intuitive and creative powers."[75]

Ask yourself some questions and then see what your intuition has to say. You can record the answers by writing in a journal or speaking into a tape recorder. Here are some questions that are similar to the earlier goal-setting exercise in Chapter 3, but this time, they are geared specifically for thinking about your work.

Questions you can ask yourself to help you decide what you want to do next:

- What do you want? Make a list of all the things you can think of. Be expansive, outrageous. Ignore or write down any negative thinking about how you can't have or don't deserve this. (If you don't know what you want, answer the next question first and then come back to this one.)

- What don't you want to do anymore?

Now pick one item from your want list and answer the following questions with it in mind.

1. What will you have to pay (sacrifice) to get what you want?

2. What might get in the way or be an obstacle to getting what you want?

3. What are your "Evil Secrets?"

   David Maister used the term "Evil Secrets" for thoughts we don't like to own, but he says it's important to acknowledge and honor them:

   "One key to discovering what you really like and love is to ask yourself what are the things you don't like to admit. 'I don't like to admit it, but I need to be the center of attention.' O.K., find a career path that will let you show off. 'I don't like to admit it, but I don't like dealing with other people.' OK, then devise a role that will let you make your contribution through things done in your office, such as intellectual

---

74 Whyte, David, *Crossing the Unknown Sea*, p. 172

75 Day, *Practical Intuition for Success*, p.4.

creativity and true technical superiority. 'I don't like to admit it, but I really want
to be rich.' Fine, go out and build a business. 'I don't like to admit it, but I'm an
intellectual snob.' That's all right, so find a career path that will allow you to work
only with smart people. Play to your 'evil secrets.' Don't suppress them. You are a lot
less flexible than you think."[76]

4. Picture yourself already having what you want. What do you see? Write it out. You don't have to think about it all the time. God is in charge of whether it is the right thing for you. Sometimes she/he says no. Sometimes she/he sends something better.

5. What one thing could you do today that would move you toward your goal?

Here are my answers to the questions:

- **What do you want?** Stay healthy. Finish this book. Keep my job. Do more telephone career counseling. Do one on-site program a month. Family members be healthy and get the things they want in life. No wars.

- **What don't you want to do anymore?** Worry about how I can never again have an empty email box as long as I have a job. Be project chair for one of the 3 major meetings — not the best use of my talents.

Pick one item from your want list and answer the following questions with it in mind.

1. What will I have to pay (sacrifice) to get what I want? To finish book, I will need to write 3 pages every morning and write the first 2 hours each weekend day.

2. What might get in the way or be an obstacle? Laziness, dusting minute corners of the house that I never look at unless I am procrastinating about writing, thinking negative thoughts — the words aren't good enough, who would care anyway, and on and on.

3. What are your evil secrets? I want to be adored by everyone. What else can I say? That covers a multitude of sins.

4. Picture yourself already having what you want. The paperback book is in airport news stands and selling well.

5. What one thing could you do today to move you toward your goal. Write 3 pages of something — more if you can get yourself to do it.

---

[76] Maister, *True Professionalism*, p.34.

Timothy Gallwey has a cautionary note about picturing what you want:

> *"When it comes to setting goals, some people say, 'You can have anything you set your mind to. You can have whatever you can imagine you can have.' He is very cautious about statements like that because when he looks back on his life and considers the events, the people, even the circumstances, that he values the most, very few of them are things that he could ever have imagined.*[77]

It is true that many wonderful things have happened that I could not have imagined, and I am ever so grateful for them. My boss has allowed me to work from a home office for over 15 years, travel to the main office when needed, and travel all over the country teaching programs. I could not have imagined such an arrangement.

But it is also true that good things happened after I wrote them down. Sometimes they occurred months or years after I wrote them down and forgot about them — my first full-time salary after having children. I wrote it in my journal and thought it was outlandishly high. It was offered to me three years after I wrote it in my journal.

Putting a goal on paper helps it come to fruition. Day says,

> *"Be sure to write it down, as opposed to 'keeping it in your head.' The mind is a very disorderly place. If you write something down, it begins to exist. You know where to find it, what to do with it. You can take it out of the messiness of the mind."*[78]

When you put it on paper, your brain thinks it, your hand writes it, your eyes see it, and then your subconscious and the universe begin to plan ways to make it happen.

Satisfaction with your work life is an important goal to strive for. Think about the activities that make you happy and that you feel are making a valuable contribution to the world. Work hard enough to do your job well, but also take time off and play in ways that are renewing to you.

---

[77] Gallwey, quote and paraphrase from *The Inner Game of Work*, p.28

[78] Day, *Practical Intuition for Success*, p.96.

Works Cited

Cameron, Julia. *The Artist's Way: A Spiritual Path to Higher Creativity*. New York: Jeremy P. Tarcher/Putnam, a member of Penguin Putnam, Inc., 1992.

Day, Laura. *Practical Intuition for Success*. New York: HarperCollinsPublishers, 1997.

Gallwey, W. Timothy. *The Inner Game of Work*. New York: Random House Trade Paperbacks, 2000.

Gillies, Jerry. *Money-Love*. New York: Warner Books, Inc., 1978.

Lamont, Anne. *bird by bird, Some Instructions on Writing and Life*. New York: Anchor Books, Doubleday, 1994.

Linney, Barbara. "What To Do Next," *Physician Executive Journal*. Tampa, FL: American College of Physician Executives, May/June 1998.

Maister, David H. *True Professionalism*. New York: The Free Press, 1997.

Richardson, Cheryl. *LifeMakeovers*. New York: Broadway Books, 2000.

Schein, Edgar H., Ph.D. *Career Anchors*. San Diego: DBM Publishing, Pfeiffer & Co., 1990

Sher, Barbara. *I Could Do Anything If I Only Knew What It Was*. New York: A Dell Trade Paperback, 1994.

Terkel, Susan and Larry. *Small Change*. New York; Jeremy P. Tarcher/Penguin, 2004.

Whyte, David. *Crossing the Unknown Sea: Work as a Pilgrimage of Identity*. New York: Riverhead Books, 2001.

Whyte, David. *The Heart Aroused, Poetry and the Preservation of the Soul in Corporate America*. New York: Currency Doubleday, 1994.

Chapter 7

Control What You Think

Left unattended my brain will think all manner of negative thoughts. I discovered there is a way to keep that from happening. Other people just choose to think about happy things and be optimistic. I did not know I had a choice, but I learned I did in 1984.

I had my first panic attack in 1982 — a month after I finished getting a Master of Arts in English. The thesis was written and the oral exams were over. In the middle of the night I awakened from a dream about being in a coffin, jumped up in a cold sweat, and ran to the window to see if the outside was still there. My heart was pounding, and I was soaked with sweat. I was surprised because the pressure to graduate was over, and I was wracked with anxiety when I was on vacation and supposedly relaxing. Much later when I looked back on that time I made sense of what happened with this thought — I had been push- ing my mind and body to do, do, do for a long time. When I let up, my whole system seemed to recoil into panic.

I did not know the name of what had happened to me — a panic attack — but I had sev- eral more over the next two years.

In 1983 I moved from a city I loved, Charlotte, North Carolina, to one I didn't, Or- lando, Florida, because my husband wanted the challenge of a new and different career. I did not want to go, but I agreed to go. I was sad and angry for a year blaming my misery on his desire to take a new job. I have always been a worrier. Add sadness and anger to worry, and you have a petri dish growing anxiety and depression.

A friend, who is a therapist, gently said to me about every six months, "I have this friend who had panic attacks and she got relief from an audiotape program." I would be polite and say to myself — "Yea, yea, yea. You don't know what I'm talking about here. When

I drive or ride in a car, I imagine the cars are going to cross the line and drive into me head on. Nobody else does that."

I also was suffering more than ever with allergies after the move to Florida. A doctor prescribed Entex LA, a horse-size, blue decongestant pill. When the allergies continued to worsen she said, "Take another one at night." I went eight days without sleep.

Nearly crazy with fatigue, I called my therapist friend and said, "Tell me more about your friend and the audiotape program." I went to see her friend and got the details on a program called CHAANGE.[79] It was a 15-week program that could change what goes on inside your head. She described what had been her symptoms and said, "This program will fix you and you don't have to believe it will. You just have to do what it says."

I mailed my $400 check. The program instructions came. They were, "Listen to a counseling audiotape you will receive in the mail every week, and listen to a 10-minute relaxation audiotape 20 times a day. I was astounded. In the past I had listened to numerous relaxation tapes one time and said, "Well, that didn't work."

Twenty times a day. Ten of those times I would actually do the progressive muscle relaxation — lie down, tense my arms and then relax, tense my shoulders and then let them go, moving through all muscle sets while breathing deeply and evenly. The other ten times I walked around with a head set on listening to the tape.

The goal was to reprogram my brain. Since mine, when left free to roam, scans the horizon looking for things to worry about, I had to occupy it with something else. The intent was to replace all the negative chatter that went on in my head with the relaxation script and also teach my body how to relax itself. It worked. Telling myself or having others tell me to just stop worrying had done no good. Replacing the worry with relaxation exercises and positive statements changed my life.

The weekly counseling tape kept saying, "We know you think listening to the relaxation tape is ridiculous. We know you think it won't help. We don't care. Do it anyway. You won't see any improvement until about seven weeks have passed." I was desperate and when I am, I follow directions when someone promises improvement.

I also stopped taking decongestants and changed to more antihistamines to treat my allergies. I stopped drinking all caffeine and alcohol. I learned caffeine in bodies prone to panic attacks is like taking poison. I was also reminded that alcohol is a depressant, and I did not want more depression from any source.

---

79 CHAANGE, www.chaange.com, 619-425-3992

That Fall I started a PhD program in English a 100 miles from home. I listened to the relaxation tape in the car. It allowed me to drive more comfortably, and I was so wired there was no danger that it would put me to sleep.

Just as the tape predicted, I began to improve seven weeks into the program. I was generally relaxed — not a sensation I had much experience with. After several weeks I was sent a positive statement to repeat to myself at the end of the relaxation exercise. I got an additional affirmation each week until I had five. They were: I enjoy being free of worry, fear, and anxiety. I enjoy every day. I like knowing I have a choice about how I live and how I study. I enjoy the challenge of practicing new behavior. I like being in charge of my life.

I needed to add a sentence that brought my religious beliefs into it, so my final statement is — Christ is with me. Maybe yours is "Nature strengthens me."

Twenty repetitions a day so ingrained the statements in my head that when I got up during the night to go to the bathroom, I automatically said them. I was literally reprogramming my brain. I know it sounds impossible, but I could feel it working.

I repeated the phrase, "I enjoy the challenge of practicing new behavior," so often that I went parasailing on vacation. I walked in the hotel room alone after checking in, looked out the window, and saw two men hooking a person into the harness attached to the sail. I put on my bathing suit and went straight down to the beach. The small motor boat pulled me high over the blue waters of Acapulco. I bought the pictures to prove it. No one would have believed I would do such a thing.

Many psychological sources say the first sentence of the six affirmations should not be about anxiety — if you mention anxiety, you are going to feel it, just as saying to yourself — don't think about an elephant instantly makes you think about one. However, that did not prove true for me. I had many fears in my head all the time and saying, "I enjoy being free of worry, fear and anxiety" when one popped up would immediately cancel it. The CHAANGE therapists knew that those prone to anxiety worried about everything so the first sentence had to be a stop sign for that all-consuming habit. If life is going well, I can skip that statement and begin with, "I enjoy every day."

When you start saying affirmations, they feel like lies. Samuel Taylor Coleridge said reading literature requires a "willing suspension of disbelief."[80] This exercise needs the same behavior. With enough repetition, the positive statements become true even though they are not true in the beginning.

---

80 Coleridge, "Biographia Literaria, Chapter XIV". *The Norton Anthology of English Literature*, p.240.

In 1987 my job changed from being a college professor teaching Freshman English and Business Writing to being a consultant who traveled all over the United States teaching Business Writing and Communication Skills for the American Management Association. One of my fears was flying; so, in the taxi on the way to the airport and then on the plane, I would put the head set on and listen to the relaxation tape. I used the tape so much in those early days of more frequent flying that I established a habit of falling asleep when the plane takes off. Twenty years later, when the plane lifts off into that slanted upward position, I often fall asleep and don't wake up till the drink cart comes.

After the 15-week program in 1984, I have never had to listen to the tapes 20 times a day again, but when life has new, intense positive or negative stress, I have to start the relaxation exercises again and trot out the affirmations. I needed them the months before my son got married — a truly happy event. I needed them when his bride of seven weeks had to have surgery.

In the Fall of 1999 when my daughter was struggling with her first semester in business school, I taught her the affirmations. She and I are so different I wondered if they would work for her, but they did, and she learned to calm herself. She says they helped her do well in school. She uses the affirmations to this day and helps many of her clients to use these same affirmations or to think of their own.

Something is going on in our heads all the time. Have you ever watched the movies in your mind? You can see the color red in an advertisement on the side of a bus, remember you had a red wagon when you were six, that your brother knocked you out of it and in ten seconds be instantly angry. In *Coping Better...Anytime Anywhere*, Maultsby says this constant thinking and reacting is self counseling — "the only means of self-control for everybody...as long as you are awake and alert, you will have to counsel yourself. Your only choice will be how you do it."[81]

The relaxation exercise and positive statements enable me to take control of that self-counseling and say better things to myself. On one of our annual, mountain vacations my husband mentioned that he memorized hundreds of hymns as a result of going to church in his growing up years on Sunday morning, Sunday night, and Wednesday night. He said the hymns pop up in his head all the time. It helps explain to me his cheerfulness and hopeful outlook on life. They are his affirmations.

The affirmations also help me listen to others who are having struggles in their lives without absorbing too much of their pain. It is important for me to remember that whatever

---

81 Maultsby, *Coping Better...Anytime Anywhere*, pp.4-5.

atrocious things are happening in the world, whatever difficulties my family members are experiencing are not necessarily my fault, and even if they are, I can't fix them.

The CHAANGE therapists described the importance of having appropriate defenses. Terrible things happen every day and most people manage to go on with their lives because they have defenses — the ability to ignore them. Lou Owensby, one of the counselors in the CHAANGE program, said it takes energy to hold up your defenses — about the same amount of energy it would take to hold an air-filled beach ball under water at the ocean. People who are spending all their time worrying don't have the energy to hold up their defenses. They have to learn or remember to do it. If I am overly anxious, I don't read the newspaper or watch the news on TV. I don't watch violent movies because the images get in my system, cause me physical pain, and I can dream about them for months.

I am the most productive and happy when I do a relaxation exercise or listen to a meditation CD before I get out of bed in the morning, then write in my journal for 15 minutes before the work day begins, and walk 30 minutes at the end of the day.

If you want to give some of this a try, but it seems like way too much work or your needs are less than mine, try small bits of what I did and see what works best for you. Start by paying attention to your breathing. Maxie Maultsby says you can change how you feel in minutes by saying and doing, " I am breathing in. I am breathing out. I am relaxed."[82]

Buy just the relaxation tape from the CHAANGE organization and listen to it once a day for 3 weeks.[83] You won't be able to change a habit without at least three weeks of practice. When you finish the relaxation exercise say to yourself an affirmation, a positive statement that applies to your life situation. You may be thinking your symptoms are not as bad as mine. If they are not, this process can still add pleasure and creativity to your life.

Here are some affirmations that Julia Cameron recommends: "My creativity heals myself and others. There is a divine plan of goodness for me...and for my work. I am willing to be of service through my creativity."[84] Others: I am happy and healthy. I enjoy my work.

Develop affirmations for yourself by thinking about what is wrong with your life and then by coming up with a phrase that is a positive, problem-solved statement. "An affirmation is a strong, positive statement about something that is already so."[85] It will not be true in the beginning, but you have the best chance of its becoming true if you will repeat it to yourself over and over.

---

82 Maultsby, *Coping Better... Anytime Anywhere*, p.35.

83 CHAANGE, www.chaange.com, 619-425-3992

84 Cameron, *The Artist's Way*, pp.36-37.

85 Shakti Gawain in Cameron's *The Artist's Way*, p.37.

Fifteen minutes of freewriting in the morning can help you identify the problems and come up with a positive take on them. Cameron says, "Every morning, set your clock one-half hour early; get up and write three pages of longhand, stream of consciousness morning writing."[86] If that seems too much, then to get started write two pages any time of day three days a week.

Knowing what works, I still have a hard time getting myself to begin again when life stresses increase. I'll think it won't work this time, and for a while, I would rather rehearse a wrong done to me and play out righteous indignation in my head. How could so and so say/do such and such? They are wrong, and I am right. The first dozen or so times of that little drama, I feel superior, better than the person I am thinking about, but eventually I begin to feel sad. At that point, I can continue to wallow in it, or I can choose something else. I can decide to take control of my mind and every time the negative thought pops in my head, I can stop it and say, "I enjoy being free of worry, fear, and anxiety. I enjoy every day. I like knowing I have a choice about how I live and how I study. I enjoy the challenge of practicing new behavior. I like being in charge of my life. Christ is with me."

This process seems simplistic and too easy to possibly work. It is, in fact, very difficult to make myself do it, but when I do, it works. Most of the time I choose to do it.

Eckhart Tolle and Oprah in their webcast to millions in March 2008 described how important it is to live in the present moment. Be here right now — not in the past or in the future. I agree with the concept but find it very hard to sustain. I can make the shift when I am reading my underlined sentences in Eckhart's book[87] or when I am watching their conversation on my computer. When I am out and about, it is harder. My affirmations bring me back to the present — particularly the first two. I enjoy being free of worry fear, and anxiety. I enjoy every day.

Frederick Buechner has a paragraph in *Telling Secrets* that helps me to do the work of choosing what I think. He described a rule he had been following. I read it and thought — me, too.

> "...a rule that I had...laid down for myself was: that I had no right to be happy unless the people I loved – especially my children – were happy too. I have come to believe that that is not true. I believe instead that we, all of us, have not only the right to be happy no matter what but also a kind of sacred commission to be happy – in the sense of being free to breathe and move, in the sense of being able to bless

---

86 Cameron, p. 37

87 Tolle, Eckhart, *A New Earth: Awakening to Your Life's Purpose*

our own lives, even the sad times of our own lives, because through all our times we can learn and grow, and through all our times, if we keep our ears open, God speaks to us his saving word. Then by drawing on all those times we have had, we can sometimes even speak and live a saving word to the saving of others. I have come to believe that to be happy inside ourselves...is in the long run the best we can do both for ourselves and for the people closest to us. If we do it right, maybe they can be helped to be a little stronger through our strength, maybe even a little happier through our happiness."[88]

Learning a way to control what I think has enabled me to thoroughly enjoy life when things are good and cope better when they are not. I truly did not realize I had a choice. I thought whatever was going on in my head was just the way my brain worked.

First relaxation audio tapes helped me change my thinking, then a specific hypnosis tape tailored to my needs by a counselor I was working with and now a meditation CD with the sounds of gongs, rain and binaural beats.[89] If I am listening to something with a headset that tells me what to do step-by-step, I obey. The rest and relief are wonderful. If the sources I've suggested don't seem right for you, go online and type in Guided Relaxation.

If I practice being aware of my breathing, I feel calmer. If I say my affirmations, I feel better. Everything I read and hear tells me people are trying to manage time and stress, to find joy and meaning. I believe these tools will help you do that.

---

88 Buechner, *Telling Secrets*, p.102.

89 "Awakening Prologue," The Holosync Solution, Disc Two, www.centerpointe.com.

Works Cited

Buechner, Frederick. *Telling Secrets*. SanFrancisco: HarperSanFrancisco, 1991.

Cameron, Julia. *The Artist's Way*. New York: Jeremy P. Tarcher/Putnam, 1992.

CHAANGE, www.chaange.com, 619-425-3992.

Coleridge, Samuel Taylor. "Biographia Literaria, Chapter XIV," *The Norton Anthology of English Literature*, Vol. 2. New York: W. W. Norton & Co, Inc., 1962.

Maultsby, Maxie C., Jr., M.D. *Coping Better... Anytime Anywhere*. Bloomington, Indiana: Rational Self-Help Books, 1986.

The Holosync Solution, Disc Two, "Awakening Prologue," www.centerpointe.com.

Tolle, Eckhart. *A New Earth: Awakening to Your Life's Purpose*. New York: A Plume Book, 2005.

Chapter 8

Dance When You Can

Whatever brings you joy, find a way to do it. I love to dance. If I can get my body to move with the rhythm of the music, I feel free, beautiful, at one with God. I am using the phrase as a metaphor for any activity that is fun, renews your spirit, makes you feel connected to your Creator.

I have discussed ways to take care of yourself, communicate with others, set goals, tap your creativity, and be productive. Now let's concentrate on having fun, remembering to reconnect with your God, and ways to reach out to others.

What do you do for fun? If you have trouble answering the question, ask yourself this — What did you like to do when you were 5, 6, 7, 8 or 15? Are you doing anything related to those activities now? What was fun? I didn't know the answer to that question the first time I asked myself or the tenth time I asked, but I kept asking and eventually ideas came to me. I love to read, write, paint, sew, knit and dance. When I have free time, I recite this list and pick one I'd like to do. For each activity the seed of desire was planted when I was between five and eight, but grew as I got older. Following are examples of some memories in hopes that they will help you think of your ways to have fun.

My Fun Activities

Reading

My love of reading began when I was five. I begged my mother to teach me to read when my older brother was sick with the flu, and she was helping him with his homework. She did. I remember the blue and red primers — Dick and Jane. See Spot run. She bought workbooks with cute little drawings of apples, cats, and dogs for me to write letters, then words. When school began, I was ahead of everyone else in the first grade and reading became a forever activity.

Writing

An event that fueled my love of paper was an altercation with my Daddy when I was in the second grade. I wanted two-25 cent packs of paper from his grocery store so my notebook would be thick like the big kids on the bus. He said I could only have one. I said, "If I can't have two, I don't want any," and I sashayed back into the store to put them down. When I came back out, he had pulled a slab off an orange crate he was breaking down and popped me on the bottom. It is the only spanking I ever got from him, but I also didn't sass him any more. To this day I write on five-subject, spiral notebooks because I like how thick they are.

School always required writing, especially since I was an English major in college, but I did not experience it as fun until graduate school when my favorite professor taught me about freewriting.

Knitting

Agnes, my grown-up friend across the street in Port Royal, Virginia, who always invited me over, taught me to knit when I was six. Following an intricate pattern with a magnifying rod, I made a baby's blue sweater with white elephants knitted in. Whatever mistakes I made in the sweater, she would fix at night, and then I'd knit more sitting beside her the next day.

Painting

Each week in Sunday school, we received a one-page folded lesson with a picture on the front — things like Jesus holding a lamb or Zaccheus in the tree trying to get Jesus' attention. I would try to draw the picture. Sometimes I got it pretty close to looking like the picture. I always liked arts and crafts — fixing bulletin boards in school, copying pictures of flowers, landscapes, animals.

When I was a junior in college, I wanted to take 17 hours the first semester. I had the five core academic courses of 15 hours lined up, but then I was looking for an extra, easy 2 hours. A friend who had been my junior counselor the year before said, "Take studio art." I said, "You must be kidding." She said, "If you do your 30 sketches a month and try everything the professor suggests, she will give you a B. You will never get an A — only the art majors get A's." She added, "There is one drawback. The oil paints and brushes will cost you $25." In 1965 that made me pause, but I took the course. It was one of the most wonderful things I have ever done for myself. I have continued to paint and often create paintings to go in specific places as I decorated my houses over the years. My daughter often asks me to paint things for her home and office.

Sewing

When I was in high school and college, Villager, John Meyer and McMullen were the brand names of stylish A-lined skirts, sleeveless shift dresses, round-collared blouses, shirt dresses, and cable sweaters. I could buy two outfits and then had to make the rest if I wanted more. My mother taught me to sew in the summer time, and sewing was part of a Home Economics course I took my senior year when I dropped physics. (My guidance counselor did not approve.) I perfected the talent the first year I was married when I realized I did not have money to buy clothes beyond what I had brought with me as the traditional trousseau — a year's worth of clothing. I wanted more.

Dancing

I first danced with Agnes's younger, handsome grown-up brother when I was six. While I stood on his feet, he moved me around the room. In the 6th grade I taught myself to dance holding onto my bed post and looking in the floor length mirror on my closet door. A blonde, blue-eyed, bronze-skinned lifeguard had asked me to dance at a pool party. I did not know how to dance, but I didn't intend to let that happen twice.

My first husband would dance. My second will not and after a failed first marriage, I learned dancing was not high on my prioritized list of qualities I wanted in a mate. I still love dancing so I learned to dance alone in my basement. The music and the dancing lift my spirits. I pretend I'm dancing with some past good partners or sometimes I imagine dancing with God.

Remembering to Reconnect to Your God

I want to say more about God and the spiritual life with no thought that I have all the answers for your life, but to encourage you to look for your own meaning and occasional answers. I believe it is important to acknowledge there is a higher power no matter what name you use — God, Universe, Nature, the Force, the Collective Unconscious. Life and all its challenges will improve if you get quiet, turn within, turn your face toward God, figure out what you want, try to understand what she/he wants for you. It simply is not an area to skip if you are looking for some measure of contentment during the good times and help during the rough spots. Being tuned into God brings me peace. Without it none of the rest of what I've suggested works for me.

Robin Norwood, in *Women Who Love Too Much* wrote,

> *"If you are on the fence about whether there is any such thing as a higher power in the universe, you might want to try acting as if you did believe even if you don't...If you have an active faith, and you regularly worship and frequently pray, developing your spirituality may mean trusting that what is happening in your life has its own reason and its own results, and that God is in charge...not you....ask for guidance in how to live your own life while you release those around you to live theirs."*[90]

When I was 24 my first husband left me. I thought I would die from the pain and shame. On that first day of separation I said, "God if you are really there, show me now — give me five minutes of relief from this pain." I got the five minutes of relief before the next wave of misery. There have been many other times since then when I asked for help and received it. In 2000 I was given strength to do something I thought I could not possibly do — break down my mother's house of 43 years in one weekend after I moved her to a retirement community. The strong arms of one of her caretakers did the lifting as I made hundreds of decisions about what went where.

What I've always wanted is a billboard sign on the side of the road with a message from God that says in HUGE letters — "Barbara, Do this now and everything will be all right." It is not what I get, but I do get something — a slight direction, a sense of the next thing to do. I can more clearly see that God was at work when I look backward than when I look forward. Knowing God will always be there when I look forward requires faith.

In 1982 I began my thesis for a MA in English with these words: "I would like to dance through my life with faith more often my partner than fear. Since death is the wallflower ever looking for a companion, I want to bow to tragedy for only the time it takes to heal and go on."[91] To live in faith more often than fear is always a goal for me.

Prayer

I pray all the time, but it seems presumptuous to talk about it. I get strength and courage from it, but often feel I don't know how to do it. Here is what I do. Every day I begin my morning pages with Dear God. I had been doing this for a couple of years before *The Color Purple* was published. I was very secretive about it and was blown away when I opened the book and saw that Alice Walker had started every chapter that way. It helped me come out of hiding about the process.

---

[90] Norwood, *Women Who Love Too Much*, pp.234-235.

[91] Linney, *The Chosen Self Dances in a Writing Class*, p.1

I begin: Dear God, Thank you for the sleep, for this new day, for good health, for letting me live with this man in this house in this city. For letting me know and love my children and now my daughter-in-law and grandchildren. For a mother who loves me dearly. For meaningful work. For my friends, church, community, country, world. Please take care of all of them.

I tell her/him what is on my mind, big stuff — please heal my grandson. Little stuff — I still miss having a cup of tea. Sometimes an answer seems to come while I'm writing. Sometimes later.

I ask God to show me what she/he would have me do this day and give me the wisdom to know what it is and the courage to do it. I ask for my loved ones to be healthy, get what they want and also be serving you. I ask for world peace. I used to plead for the Vietnam War to be over. It finally was, but there has always been a war somewhere to pray about. When I said my prayers as a child, I said "God bless — a list of people and then God bless everyone else." It is still what I revert to when I am overwhelmed by the world's problems and can't figure out how to pray about them.

During the workday when I am overwhelmed with too many emails and too many projects, I pray — help me decide the next most important thing to do. After the tragedy of 9/11 and during the economic down turn that followed, there was a first round of layoffs in my organization. I prayed — help me do the work and not worry about the possibility of the next round. When I walk at night, I say thank you for letting me eat, sleep, breathe, walk and talk.

I try to let go and put things in God's hands. On good days I can do it. On bad days, I beg for what I want. I wince when I remember that I asked him to change answers on tests when I was in college. Sometimes it seemed to happen. When I have had times of nausea and throwing up, I promise anything if she/he will make it stop. When I, my children, or loved ones are hurting, I beg for the pain to stop.

My prayers can go from begging to telling God how best to solve a problem. A prayer I say regularly to help me stop that came from the *Power of Positive Thinking*,

> *I put myself, my family, my business, my future in your hands — whatever you say goes. I don't even know how You are going to tell me what to do, but I am ready to hear and will follow Your advice if You will make it clear.*[92]

---

[92] Paraphrased from Peale, *Power of Positive Thinking*, p.39.

I ask God for what I want but also ask her/him to help me stand, accept or rejoice over what I get. Since none of us gets out of life alive, eventually some heart-breaking times will come. I try hard not to worry about the rough times before they come. It has been a life-long struggle for me because worry is my automatic default setting. There have been times in church when I listened to the confession of sins, and thought I just didn't do that much mean this week, but one day it dawned on me that excessive worry was sin and a lack of faith. My daily sin, as daily a temptation as an alcoholic who craves a drink, is to worry and try to control events in the world and in my family. I need forgiveness for it every day, and I need God's help to stop it. I'm better than I used to be.

I keep several quotes close by to remind me to let God be in charge:

Frederick Buechner

> "Stop trying to protect, to rescue, to judge, to manage the lives around you – your children's lives, the lives of your husband, your wife, your friends – because that is just what you are powerless to do. Remember that the lives of other people are not your business. They are their business. They are God's business because they all have God whether they use the word God or not. Even your own life is not your business. It also is God's business. Leave it to God. It is an astonishing thought. It can become a life-transforming thought."[93]

Melody Beattie

> "I believe that clutching tightly to a person or thing, or forcing my will on any given situation eliminates the possibility of my Higher Power doing anything constructive about that situation, the person, or me. My controlling blocks God's power. It blocks other people's ability to grow."[94]

Robin Norwood

> "Find out what brings you peace and serenity and commit some time, at least half an hour daily, to that practice. You must accept the fact that you may not know what is best in a given situation either for yourself or for another person....Letting go of self-will means becoming willing to hold still, be open, and wait for guidance for yourself."[95]

These quotes remind me God is in charge, and they help me loosen my grip on an outcome I've decided is the only right one.

---

[93] Buechner, *Telling Secrets*, p.92.

[94] Beattie, *Co-Dependent No More*, p.80.

[95] Norwood, *Women Who Love Too Much*, p.235.

Giving

Give some talent away. An essential component of the spiritual life is giving to others. Whatever you do best – the special talents that you are paid for in your work – sometimes give them away for free. I have taught the Myers-Briggs Type Indicator, presentation skills, writing classes, speaking and listening skills, and how to run an effective meeting to church groups over the years.

Give some money away. You will feel better and have expressed gratitude for the privilege of being alive. Many religious traditions say give ten percent. United Way offers everyone an opportunity to give. Many organizations work together to build Habitat for Humanity houses.

Give some time away. You give of yourself when you offer your undivided attention to your spouse, child, grandchild, aging parents, friend, co-worker. You stop what you are doing, turn your face to them and listen for the length of time you've decided you can. People are emotionally fed when they are listened to. It doesn't have to be all day long or every day. A half hour or an hour of rapt attention can satisfy a person's longing to be acknowledged and heard. It is a tremendous gift. Family members will thrive if they know they will receive that kind of listening from you on a regular basis. For a child it could be a half hour a day, for a spouse a date every weekend.

Take each child out to eat separately and regularly, sit across the table from him or her and listen. Even teenagers want to go out to eat, and they may tell you a few things if you don't tell them how to run their lives but just listen over lunch.

Anne Morrow Lindbergh in *Gift from the Sea* described the fact that we all want to be someone's "one and only" love. That is impossible, but we can have "one and only" moments when we have another person's undivided attention.[96] It is the level of concentration and the dependable regularity of it that is life saving. After reading that book, my husband and I began to take our daughter and son on individual trips so they had "one and only moments" with each of us.

Carve Out a Space for Yourself

To turn your face to God, to pray, some alone time is essential. When my children were very little, they would wake up about 5:00 am. I started getting up at 4:00 am so I could have an hour of alone time before the day began.

---

[96] Lindbergh, *Gift From the Sea*, pp.71-73.

When they were eight and ten, we moved to Florida, and I lost my alone time space. My husband was taking a job he had long dreamed about. While I did not want to go, I said yes in May and we moved in August. I was in an emotional fog during the house-hunting trip and the move. We had bought a Florida style house — open everything — the kitchen blends into a great room and flows into the living room area, tall ceilings, angled rooms. (Truthfully, I like symmetrical box shaped houses, with rectangular rooms, all ceilings the same height and a door for privacy on every room.) I had the presence of mind to insist that a kitchen door be installed so I could keep the dog from having free roaming space, but beyond that I just let things happen.

After several months I looked around and realized not one area of the house was mine alone. My husband had claimed the guest bedroom as his office and had his huge roll top desk put in there, but he actually did his work in a chair in our bedroom. The children each had a room of their own with a door that closed. The den and the kitchen were open air and together.

I announced one day — "I want a room of my own with a door and a lock on it." There were harsh words, and I left in a huff and drove to the mall. When I came back two hours later, the roll top desk had been moved to our bedroom. The glamorous white tile in its path had been scuffed, and I did not care. I could not imagine that one person could move that desk, but he had moved it. From then on the guest bedroom was all mine.

I had said what I meant and got a long-lasting fabulous result. On his next work trip he brought back a small wood-carved sign that said, "The Office" to put on the wall. Virginia Woolf said all women writers need a room of their own. I've had one ever since.

If a room of your own is not possible, drive your car to a safe parking lot and eat lunch alone. If you do not have a car, go for a walk alone.

Claiming some space can be an announcement to family members that change is coming. Being able to get away, be by yourself, not be watched and commented on is healing. In the quiet, thank God for your blessings. Ask for help with your troubles. Try to listen for the things you are called to do.

Relaxation and Meditation

One of the important things to do alone is relax. I've read 10-15 books on relaxation and meditation. The underlying theme of all of them is slow breathing, which seems insultingly simple but is unbelievably difficult to do if you are not relaxed. As I mentioned earlier, Maxie Maultsby says you can make yourself feel better in 2-5 minutes under any circumstances if you take control of your breathing. Every time I come to that advice I think — oh that again.

I cannot do it without the aid of a headset and the current technology — cassette player, then CD, now MP3 player. The longest I've ever meditated on my own is a week. But I've listened to deep relaxation audiotapes and a meditation CD every day for months at a time. Some were generic ones that anyone can buy.

Others were made for me personally by a counselor, and they helped me with a specific challenge at the time, but had the side effect of creating a sense of well-being and more relaxed breathing throughout the day. Because I am over 50, I needed to have a base-line colonoscopy to screen for cancer. I had been putting it off because I thought the prep would aggravate a digestive problem I sometimes have.

I went to a counselor who had been trained in hypnosis and said, "I have to go through a medical procedure that I think will have bad side effects on my body." Can hypnosis help keep that from happening? She said, "I think so. It has helped others." So I explained my situation. She did the hypnosis session and recorded it on an audiotape. I listened to the tape every day from September to January. It was deep relaxation with positive suggestions for healing. I found I felt better in all ways in about two weeks — more energy and at the same time more calmness. I made it through the procedure fine — explosive preparation but when it was over, it was over — no lingering side effects.[97]

Reaching Out to Others

I listen for God when I'm alone, but I also listen for God's words spoken by other people. When I first started my consulting business in 1987, I was in New York taking a four-day business writing course taught by the American Management Association. I was terrified that I would not be able to teach the course two months later. At lunch time I wandered into St. Patrick's Cathedral. I was raised Baptist and the voice of my relatives rang in my ears — something bad could happen to me for just being in a Catholic church. I sat down for noon-day mass and the priest said, "Consecrated means holy, set apart for a special purpose. God gives you the heart, mind, and spirit for the job he has given you.

---

[97] You may be skeptical about hypnosis. I was, too. I learned it is extreme relaxation with good words. I got referrals from sources I trusted for a counselor who did hypnosis. The session was recorded on an audiotape so I could listen to it at home. That also enabled me to be sure everything that was said on it was acceptable to me. I know it can be helpful in healing and changing communication patterns. Others have said it can help with weight loss and smoking cessation. Chapter 10 of the following book, "How to Select a Qualified Clinical Hypnosis Practitioner." *Hypnotize Yourself Out of Pain Now!* Bruce N. Eimer, PhD, ABPP, P. 195.

He will give you the wisdom and gentleness to do it as he would have done it."[98] I went back to the class, encouraged, thinking the message was meant for me and somehow I would figure out how to effectively teach the program. I did.

Form a Small Group

You need time alone, but you also need to be with people. Carl Jung said for the balanced life, you need to tend to the inner life and the outer life neither to the exclusion of the other. I am most comfortable tending to the inner life, but if I am going to tend to the outer life, I must be with other people.

You can form a small group (up to seven) around some issue for fun and support — a book club, a knitting circle, a golf foursome, a small religious group. Alcoholics Anonymous is probably the first and most famous group at teaching that changing behavior and getting through rough times requires listening, encouragement, and support from others. Even the good times are enriched if we have people we can share them with.

I have formed several writing groups over the years. They not only help me produce words, they give me support and a place to risk telling what is going on in my life. It's different from most writing classes because there is no criticism, only encouragement.

I start the group by explaining the freewriting process (as I did in Chapter 1) and then we do the "now moment" questions together at the first meeting. I'll list them again here, but they are discussed in detail in Chapter 5.

1. Write one thing you like about your present job (outside the home or at home).

2. Write one thing that frustrates you about your job (outside the home or at home).

3. What kinds of things are you putting your energy into now? (Either at work or away from work)

4. What kinds of things are you struggling with?

5. If you had a magic genie, what would you command it to do to solve one of your problems?

6. Who are the people who are important to you? List them and write a few things about them.

7. What are your dreams and hopes?

---

[98] Mass at St. Patrick's Cathedral in New York, June 1987.

8. Name an image or a picture that describes your life right now. (If this is hard for you, just write over and over — What is my life like? What is my life like? And see if any image comes to you. Sometimes it does and sometimes it doesn't.

9. Is there something you would like to get from this writing exercise today?

10. List some things you do to take care of yourself.

Twenty minutes of non-stop writing sets the stage. People experience the freewriting process and the self-reflective information the "now moment" questions bring up. Then I ask them to look at what they have written and see if they are willing to read any of it to the group. Some pick the low-risk topics — ways you take care of yourself. Others pick high risk — what are your hopes and dreams. Others choose not to tell anything. Any response is fine. (More details about how to run the group are in the Appendix.)

Join a Large Group

Go to church, a synagogue, a mosque, a "save the planet" group — somewhere there is a community of people who intend to do good things.

Black Elk Speaks, a book about Native Americans, describes the importance of community in helping to find the power to live into your calling. The book's character had a dream about his life's work as a shaman. The tribe's tradition was that the dream had to be acted out in his community before the spiritual power could come to him. So his tribe dressed up in decorative costumes, painted their faces and their horses, and acted out the dream just as he described it.

Afterwards he wrote,

> "...and many I cured with the power that came through me. Of course, it was not I who cured. It was the power from the outer world, and the visions and ceremonies had only made me like a hole through which the power could come to the two-leggeds. If I thought that I was doing it myself, the hole would close up and no power could come through. Then everything I could do would be foolish."[99]

As an Introvert, being in a large group is more stressful for me. I would rather be alone than engaged in the messiness of dealing with other people. However, a large group is where they are, and from time to time Introverts need community, too. I can talk to them, help them, be helped by them, worship with them.

---

[99] Neihardt, *Black Elk Speaks*, p.174.

As I mentioned in Chapter Three, Carlyle Marney, the second minister at my church, wrote about the powerful healing that can occur if you tell your story and someone listens carefully: We are all "guilty, shamed, and frightened...and almost no where dare we tell anyone about it." If you do tell and you are heard, not harshly judged forever, and loved anyway, you are "...really never again as if you have not been heard."[100]

The "being-heard" moments can happen one-on-one or in a small group. In my community the sermons on Sunday morning in the large group set the tone of acceptance and forgiveness that enable people to risk telling their stories in small groups or to have the courage for one-on-one conversations of confession with friends.

This has happened for me several times in my church community.

> *Example 1:* I said to my minister, "I shoved my five-year daughter too hard to get her where I wanted her to go. I cried. He said, "Children's House can help you," and a counselor there did. I changed how I was rearing my children. I never again almost physically abused my child. I learned ways to persuade and discipline without spanking and most of the time without screaming.

> *Example 2:* I said some harsh things to a friend that spilled out after too much silence. I had not liked some things she had been doing in a support group we were in, but I was too chicken to say so. I finally spoke up and said too much with a mean tone. She was very hurt. I wanted to reconcile. I tried calling. Twice she wouldn't come to the phone. The third time I said, "I have a pattern of not speaking up for way too long, and then I explode. I want to stop it." She said, "A personal growth lab in Richmond, Virginia, can help you," and it did.

Each time I need to speak up and risk saying what I think, I must again find the courage to do it. Because I've been listened to and forgiven for some things I've done that were inappropriate, I have the hope (not the guarantee) that it can happen again when I need it. When I left Charlotte, North Carolina, for twelve years, I took with me the knowledge that there was a place where I had been heard.

I moved back to Charlotte and the church I love in 1995. I have found it to be a community that listens compassionately when you are having troubles, calls you to change behavior, supports you while you struggle to change, and then doesn't remind you of past mistakes — a combination of confronting love and grace.

---

[100] Marney, *The Recovery of the Person*, pp.158-159.

My original family, my husband, children, daughter-in-law, and friends have listened to me. I have done the same for them and for people I work with and for. Regularly turning our faces to each other, intently listening, and saying what we mean have improved our communication and increased our creativity. Both things make me feel glad to be alive.

Works Cited

Beattie, Melody. *Codependent No More, How to Stop Controlling Others and Start Caring for Yourself.* San Francisco: HarperSanFrancisco, 1992.

Buechner, Frederick. *Telling Secrets.* San Francisco: HarperSanFrancisco, 1991.

Cameron, Julia. *The Artist's Way.* New York: Jeremy P. Tarcher/Putnam, 1992.

Eimer, Bruce N. *Hypnotize Yourself Out of Pain Now!* Oakland, CA: New Harbinger Publications, Inc., 2002.

Lindbergh, Anne Morrow. *Gift from the Sea, Twentieth Anniversary Edition.* New York: Vintage Books, A Division of Random House, 1978.

Linney, Barbara J. *The Chosen Self Dances in a Writing Class.* Charlotte, NC: UNCC Press, 1982.

Marney, Carlyle. *The Recovery of the Person.* Nashville: Abingdon Press, 1963.

Mass at St. Patrick's Cathedral, New York, June 1987.

Neihardt, John G. *Black Elk Speaks.* New York: Washington Square Press, 1959.

Norwood, Robin. *Women Who Love Too Much.* New York: Pocket Books, 1985.

Peale, Norman Vincent. *The Power of Positive Thinking,* Condensed Edition. New York: Center for Positive Thinking, 1987.

How to Form a Small Writing Group

I'll describe how I run the group just in case it's the kind of small group you would like to try. You need four to seven people in the group. Start the group by explaining the free-writing process (as I did in Chapter 1) and then write the answers to the "now moment" questions together at the first meeting. I'll list them again here, but they are discussed in detail in Chapter 5.

1. Write one thing you like about your present job (outside the home or at home).

2. Write one thing that frustrates you about your job (outside the home or at home).

3. What kinds of things are you putting your energy into now? (Either at work or away from work)

4. What kinds of things are you struggling with?

5. If you had a magic genie, what would you command it to do to solve one of your problems?

6. Who are the people who are important to you? List them and write a few things about them.

7. What are your dreams and hopes?

8. Name an image or a picture that describes your life right now. (If this is hard for you, just write over and over — What is my life like? What is my life like? And see if any image comes to you. Sometimes it does and sometimes it doesn't.

9. Is there something you would like to get from this writing exercise today?

10. List some things you do to take care of yourself.

The amount of writing the ten questions require sets the stage for how the group will work. People experience the freewriting process and the self-reflective information the "now moment" questions bring up.

Then I ask them to look at what they have written and see if they are willing to read any of it to the group. Some pick the low-risk topics – ways you take care of yourself. Others pick high risk – what are your hopes and dreams. Others choose not to tell anything. Any response is fine.

We meet once a month. I suggest that they write ten minutes of freewriting five days a week during the intervening time. I ask people to bring one page of writing with them each time we meet. Some do. Some don't. It doesn't matter. We always start the session with ten minutes of freewriting and then telling something from it if we wish.

Here's how we deal with the one page of writing if they brought one from home. The person reads it. The group members learn when they hear others read their pages aloud. They think to themselves – yes I could do that or no I wouldn't do it that way. When they read their own piece, they feel courageous for having read it. They may feel afraid, happy, sometimes tearful, but they survive the reading.

When they finish, the listeners write the answer to these two questions – What did you hear the loudest and where did you want to know more? They read their answers, and the author just listens – no defending comment such as, "This is why I did such and such."

Suppose five people hear the same thing the loudest. That is great feedback because you know that part of the writing is really getting through to people. The listener may hear an emotion rather than specific words the loudest – fear, sadness, happiness.

The reading is risky and makes you feel vulnerable, but whenever I've done it, I've produced more words that others have responded well to and that I've been proud of. Julia Cameron says: "...very often a risk is worth taking simply for the sake of taking it. There is something enlivening about expanding our self-definition, and a risk does exactly that. Selecting a challenge and meeting it creates a sense of self-empowerment that becomes the ground for further successful challenges. Viewed this way, running a marathon increases your chances of writing a full-length play. Writing a full-length play gives you a leg up on a marathon."[101]

---

[101] Cameron, *The Artist's Way*, p.123.

Here are some things not to do in the writing group: Don't allow the session to become a judgment fest. Don't correct grammar. Don't tell the writer how to fix something. Don't tell what you don't like. This group activity is a place to draw forth creativity from all the participants. Creativity does not just refer to producing poems or short stories. Creativity can be producing clear, interesting sentences on a management topic that have been sifted through your own experience. It can be an action to take to solve a personal problem.

If you start judging and fixing, the flow of creativity will dry up. If you can keep harsh judgment out of the writing group, you will have an environment in which more words will come to everyone between sessions. If one of the participants is a friend who will help you edit later, wonderful, but don't do it when the group meets.

Breinigsville, PA USA
16 September 2010
245535BV00001B/7/P